The Afrocentric Idea

Temple University Press · Philadelphia

Molefi Kete Asante

The Afrocentric Idea

Temple University Press, Philadelphia 19122
Copyright © 1987 by Temple University. All rights reserved
Published 1987
Printed in the United States of America

The paper used in this publication meets the minimum
requirements of American National Standard for Information
Sciences—Permanence of Paper for Printed Library Materials,
ANSI Z39.48-1984

Library of Congress Cataloging-in-Publication Data
Asante, Molefi K., 1942–
The Afrocentric idea.
Bibliography: p.
Includes index.
1. Africa—Civilization.
2. Philosophy, African.
3. Ethnocentrism.
I. Title.
DT14.A78   1987   960   86-30046
ISBN 0-87722-483-8 (alk. paper)

To the memory of **Cheikh Anta Diop**
and **W. E. B. Du Bois**
mountains above the valleys

Acknowledgments

I do not stand alone in this enterprise; in fact, I am supported on every side by intellectual ancestors. The tradition of David Walker, W. E. B. Du Bois, Ida B. Wells, Cheikh Anta Diop, and George James serves as my inspiration. I consider myself a "Diopian"; that is, the aim of my work is to advance the study and enhance the appreciation of the complexity and historicity of African culture. As such, I am a cultural analyst, committed to the systematic exposition of communication and cultural behaviors as they are articulated in the African world.

In granting *dobale* to the ancestors, I am not expressing a political but an intellectual orientation. While my work to this point has been towards initiating Afrocentric insights in the critical study of communication behaviors, I have always emphasized the motifs, myths, rituals, and symbols implanted in my memory through experience, training, and reading. Bowing in the direction of the principal predecessors to Afrocentric thought is a recognition that we are much like individual planets whose orbits are maintained in relation to others by the steady determinism of some powerful force.

My intellectual inclinations, stirred by a curiosity about human insensitivity, interracial hatred, and cultural bias, found their full expression in the work of the great scholars. In the stellar imaginations of Du Bois and Diop, the two major

African intellectuals of the twentieth century, my interest in the Afrocentric idea found rich materials from ancient Kemet (Egypt) and other African societies. These scholars had prepared an entire generation of African intellectuals to examine Africa by listening to the African world voice.

My inspiration has also come from other sources, too numerous to call by name. Yet I feel obliged to mention a few of them. The work of John Henrik Clarke, the unswerving genius whose encyclopedic knowledge and critical acumen are without peer in this age, has influenced my outlook on history. There are also the Afrocentricists, chief of whom are Dona Richards, Jacob Carruthers, Tsehloane Keto, Maulana Karenga, and Joseph Baldwin. I have read them all with benefit. They, among many others, have been my teachers and my friends. How much I owe to the neo-African artists and writers, such as Sonia Sanchez, Haki Madhubuti, Abdias do Nascimento, Wole Soyinka, Isidore Okpewho, Atukwei Okai, James Ravell, Thelma Ravell-Pinto, and Kariamu Welsh Asante! They have given me more of their thinking than I could ever account for in specific credits, since so much of what I have written must have come from their discussions with me.

The preparation of this manuscript has been a joint effort. Benita Brown, of the Department of African American Studies, provided drafts whenever I needed them. She has been wonderful and very agreeable when I have demanded more than seemed humanly possible. Nadia Kravchenko, the indispensable brain of the word processing center at Temple University, assisted me in maintaining a profile of efficiency when I thought everything was hopeless. The final version of this manuscript was typed by her, and her generosity is greatly appreciated.

You should know that I have poured libations to the ancestors for placing me at Temple University. I have found the University dynamic, convenient to research materials, and open to visions of the future. The Charles Blockson Afro-American Collection, a remarkable resource for scholarship, is located here, as are a number of critical Afrocentricists with whom I have interacted advantageously. Janet Francendese, of Temple University Press, has provided expert editorial guidance on the manuscript, and when we have argued, I am happy to say, it has been all within the family of ideas. An author wishes for an editor who understands the essential premises; Janet Francendese has always been there.

Kariamu, my wife, and Daahoud and Molefi Khumalo, my sons, have been remarkably critical and Afrocentric while I have spent hours at the personal computer; I thank them for their understanding.

The support I have received has been universal and unselfish, yet the mistakes and errors in this book belong neither to the ancestors nor to friends, but to me alone.

Contents

The Afrocentric Idea

Dancing between Circles
and Lines

What has fascinated me is the manner in which most of my colleagues have written theory and engaged in the social sciences in relationship to African people. They have often assumed that their "objectivity," a kind of collective subjectivity of European culture, should be the measure by which the world marches. I have seldom fallen in step, insisting (gently) that there are other ways in which to experience phenomena, rather than viewing them from a Eurocentric vantage point.

My work has increasingly constituted a radical critique of the Eurocentric ideology that masquerades as a universal view in the fields of intercultural communication, rhetoric, philosophy, linguistics, psychology, education, anthropology, and history. Yet the critique is radical only in the sense that it suggests a turnabout, an alternative perspective on phenomena. It is about taking the globe and turning it over so that we see all the possibilities of a world where Africa, for example, is subject and not object. Such a posture is necessary and rewarding for Africans and Europeans. The inability to "see" from several angles is perhaps the one common fallacy in provincial scholarship. Those who have delighted us most and advanced thought most significantly have been thinkers who explored different views and brought new perspectives.

The Eurocentric Tradition

I am inclined to think that the critical theorists, particularly those of the Frankfurt School, are engaged in a somewhat similar enterprise in re-orienting thinking. The difference, however, is profound. Jürgen Habermas, Herbert Marcuse, Theodor Adorno, and Max Horkheimer are essentially embroiled in a Eurocentric family debate over the nature of ideology. This is why Raymond Geuss could say that even Marxism and Freudian thought "exhibit such strong similarities in their essential epistemic structure that from a philosophical point of view they don't represent two different kinds of theory, but merely two instances of a single new type."[1] Whether one accepts a Marxist or Freudian view of reality, one is primarily participating in a limited view of reality. But beyond Marxism and psychoanalysis is the fact that so-called critical theory is aligned to positivism as representative of a Eurocentric way of seeing reality. Although the fundamental purpose of the Frankfurt School seems to be a sustained criticism of positivism, its emphasis on advancing a Eurocentric tradition is wedded to the same spirit that gave birth to positivism.

I am not questioning the validity of the Eurocentric tradition within its context; I am simply stating that such a view must not seek an ungrounded aggrandizement by claiming a universal hegemony, as it has frequently done in the social sciences. Both the positivists and the Frankfurt School theorists have contributed to European thinking, albeit in quite different ways. And while I sympathize with the critical theorists in regard to the philosophic error in positivism, where it is possible for a person to have poor epistemological knowledge yet be able to test and use first-order theories in natural science, I am not convinced that the critical theorists themselves fully appreciate the kind of unity expressed in the African view of reality.

They are, in essence, captives of a peculiar arrogance, the arrogance of not knowing that they do not know what it is that they do not know, yet they speak as if they know what all of us need to know. To know the African foundations of human societies would be to possess a built-in check on such arrogance. The critical theorists may not seek to manipulate the external world in the way of the positivists, but their notions of enlightenment through reflection on the subtle pressures of society tend to be totally individualistic. Reflection is a uniquely private affair. For that reason, we must at least ask whether or not there is anything in the critical theory that relates to an Afrocentric ideology. Of course, we immediately see that we have a problem with ideology. There are descriptive, programmatic, and pejorative definitions of ideology. However, in the sense that Afrocentricity proposes a cultural reconstruction that incorporates the African perspective as a part of an entire human transformation, critical theory suggests a pathway. It does not lead us down the path, because it is trapped in the quicksand of its own ethnocentric view, but its attack on the traditional ideology of empiricism is "right on."

My objective has always been a critique that propounds a cultural theory of society by the very act of criticism. In other words, to provide a radical assessment of a given reality is to create, among other things, another reality. Furthermore, any criticism of society is, definitionally, a criticism of the ruling ideology of that society. I have the insight that comes from being born black in the United States. That fact puts me in a critical mood within the intellectual and social milieu I share with Eurocentricists. As the critic, I am always seeking to create a new world, to find an escape, to liberate those who see only a part of reality. Similarly, Countee Cullen, the noted poet, could say:

> Inscrutable His ways are, and immune
> to catechism by a mind too strewn
> with petty cares to slightly understand
> what awful brain compels his awful hand.
> Yet do I marvel at this curious thing:
> to make a poet black, and bid him sing![2]

By the act of being a poet, Countee Cullen was criticizing the dominant ideology of the society. As a writer in cultural and intellectual alignment to his basic human values, he was, by definition, in defiance of an oppressive situation.

The crystallization of this critical perspective I have named *Afrocentricity*, which means, literally, placing African ideals at the center of any analysis that involves African culture and behavior.[3] For example, the communicationist who defines a speech as an uninterrupted spoken discourse demonstrates either a disregard or ignorance of the African tradition of speech, much as Leslie Fiedler showed a purely European conception of fiction when he contended that romance was a central theme in literature. Fiedler's reaction to literature was essentially a Eurocentric contextual affair.[4] Familiar with the classics of American and British literature, he apparently accepted Western literature as world-defining. An able critic of Eurocentric culture, he failed to analyze his genre from a worldwide perspective—or, at least, to leave it open. Thus, to say that romance is central to all novels is to invoke a Western literary icon for other literatures. Traditionally, African writers are not concerned with the romance variety of literature; but Fiedler, like many Eurocentric writers, gives us no caveats. We are left with his word for literature—a truncated word, parading as universal.

Charles Larson wrote a perceptive essay, "Heroic Ethnocentrism: The Idea of Universality in Literature," in which he examined the European notion of universality.[5] Larson had first come face to face with the problem of universality while teaching an English literature course in Nigeria—a good place, I might add, to come to grips with ethnocentric ideas of all kinds. Larson's students did not understand the idea of kissing in the Victorian novel, and what happened to Larson is revealing. He groped for words to explain the work of such a celebrated writer as Thomas Hardy to his African audience. He learned, of course, how culture shapes the interpretation of literature. But culture itself is shaped by the constant demands of society and the environment. Larson concluded that kissing and description have not found counterparts in the African novel—not yet, at least. He writes, "Usually, when we try to force the concept of universality on someone who is not western, I think we are implying that our own culture should be the standard of measurement."[6] Larson is correct to see Fiedler's assertion that the "love story" is universal as another Western analysis imposed on world literature. Since there are entire cultural areas where the "love story" is *non*existent, the universality of the "love story" is doubtful. There are no major African novels where the plot progresses because of a hero's attempt to attract a mate. An Afrocentric discussion of literature would guard against this ethnocentric promotion of a group universality.

The central problem with Fiedler and others who write in this vein is that, as fifteenth-century Europeans could not cease believing that the earth was the center of the universe, many today find it difficult to cease viewing European culture as the center of the social universe. Thus, the work they produce seldom considers the possibilities of other realities or, indeed, shared realities. A number of scholars have challenged such a narrow view of the arts and the social sciences. Their works speak to the abiding problem of Western formulations based on parochial observations.[7]

But Robert Armstrong declares, in a more direct way, that Europeans tend to speak as Fiedler had, tying themselves to all that is supposedly universal, because they have "an ethnocentric crypto-aesthetics" that links them to what they perceive as a "universal cultural phenomenon."[8] What is particularly troubling in these formulations by European and some African and Asian writers, who have been thoroughly trained in Eurocentrism, is that they assume that everyone else should simply acquiesce in their expansive provincialism. They not only make their arguments with a bewildering array of tropes, figures, and oxymorons, but they assert them as if there is no other reality, no other perspective.

It is striking that some feminist critics have addressed the same conceptual issue, though from a different point of view. For example, Karen Sacks has attacked social-Darwinist anthropology for its industrial-capitalist bias. In her study of six African societies, Sacks argues that anthropology's inherent hierarchical and competitive dimensions result in, as well as reinforce, beliefs in the natural superiority of men over women. According to Sacks, "the center of the struggle lies in changing institutionalized patterns of behaviors and allocations of social roles."[9] Since Marxism does not presume such inequality, Sacks extols its analytic advantages in the feminist movement: Social Darwinist and Marxist theories "are diametrically opposed ways of seeing the same social order(s), and they represent opposed class views and needs."[10] However, her argument, like those of other Marxist theorists, rests on a reaction to the industrial capitalist order and must use its language to demonstrate the opposition. Thus, though the opposition is real, the balance is weighted towards social Darwinism.

While Afrocentric thinkers must also confront presumptions of inequality, Marxism is not helpful in developing Afrocentric concepts and methods because it, too, is a product of a Eurocentric consciousness that excludes the historical and cultural perspectives of Africa. I am sympathetic to Sack's view, to the extent that she criticizes the social Darwinist perspective and attempts to find, as I have done, a way of seeing based on people's needs and experiences. But because it emerged from the Western consciousness, Marxism is mechanistic in its approach to social understanding and development, and it has often adopted forms of social Darwinism when explaining cultural and social phenomena. What makes Afrocentric concepts more inclusive is that they seek to reorient our world view in ways that challenge social Darwinism, capitalism, and most forms of Marxist theory—all of which are grounded in their own particularity. The invalidity of an idea arises, not from its exponents, but from its own fundamental flaws. This is the point at which the feminist critique converges with the Afrocentric line of reasoning. What I seek to do here is to move closer to the possibility of a post-Eurocentric idea where true transcultural analyses become possible; this can be accomplished alongside a post-male ideology as we unlock creative human potential.

Without severe criticism, the preponderant Eurocentric myths of universalism, objectivity, and classical traditions retain a provincial European cast. Scholarship rooted in such a tradition obviously lacks either historical or conceptual authenticity. The aggressive seizure of intellectual space, like the seizure of land, amounts to the aggressor occupying someone else's territory while claiming it as his own. The problem with this is that cultural analysis takes a back seat to galloping ethnocentric interpretations of phenomena.

Applied to the African world, such conceptions become limiting, restricting, and parochial. For example, a discussion of African cultural history rarely calls forth African culture in the American context when the discussion is made by Eurocentric writers. Like the literary critics, the historians would dismiss the African elements that survived and developed on the American continents as purely temporal. They would usually call it "Negro culture," or speak of "the African slave in the New World" or "Negro emancipation." The fact that the spatial referent is Africa is ignored and *Negro* becomes a crypto-term that is used to designate our degradation. In this way the Eurocentric writer ties the African to Negro, a false concept and a false history, separate from any particular spatial reality. *Negro* did not exist prior to slavery; both the term and its application were products of the social and economic context of the slave trade. Consequently, the attachment of the term *Negro* to African meant a negation of history and culture.

Furthermore, there is neither recognition of African classical thought nor of the African classical past in the Eurocentric formulations. We are essentially left with a discontinuous history and an uncertain future. The Afrocentric analysis reestablishes the centrality of the ancient Kemetic (Egyptian) civilization and the Nile Valley cultural complex as points of reference for an African perspective in much the same way as Greece and Rome serve as reference points for the European world. Thus, the Afrocentricist expands human history by creating a new path for interpretation, making words like *negro* and *colored* obsolete and anachronistic. *African* is identified with time, place, and perspective. Without the Afrocentric perspective the imposition of the European line as *universal* hinders cultural understanding and demeans humanity.

Such deliberately separatist views carry the false assertion that Africans in the Americas are not Africans connected to their spatial origin. While differences exist between Barbados and Zimbabwe, these differences are much like the differences between Florence and Brisbane. African American culture and history represent developments in African culture and history, inseparable from place and time. Analysis of African American culture that is not based on Afrocentric premises is bound to lead to incorrect conclusions. In a similar manner, the interpretation of historical data from a strictly Eurocentric perspective can lead to serious intercultural conflict, based on wrong premises.

Let me give an example of how cultural misunderstandings can be propagated on the basis of different views. In the nineteenth century, Cecil John Rhodes sought to gain control of a large territory of southern Africa, controlled by the Ndebele King Lobengula, and sent emissaries to the powerful king in an effort to secure his consent. After many days of discussion with Lobengula, the white emissaries returned to Rhodes with the signature of Lobengula on a piece of paper. They told Rhodes that the king had given Rhodes all of his territory. Rhodes sent a column of soldiers into the area with the instruction to shoot any black on sight. Thus began the country of Rhodesia.

Rhodes may have believed that King Lobengula gave him title to the land, but Lobengula never believed that he had. Two cultural views of the world clashed, and the Europeans automatically assumed the correctness of their view. An Afrocentric analysis points out that Lobengula could never have sold or given the land away, since it did not belong to him but to the ancestors and the community. He could grant Rhodes permission to hunt, to farm, and even to build a house, but not to own land. Only in this manner could the king follow the discourse of his ancestors. It took nearly one hundred years, two revolts, and a seven-year war to correct the situa-

tion. A rigid Eurocentrism made Rhodes believe that Lobengula had signed his country over to him.

Similarly, I am certain that the Indians did not believe they
had sold Manhattan Island for twenty-three dollars worth of
trinkets, no matter what the Dutch thought. Native Americans revered the land in much the same way as Africans. No
king or clan leader could sell what did not belong to him. On
the basis of European contractual custom, the Dutch may
have actually thought they were purchasing the island from
the Indians; but this was obviously a view based on their own
commercial traditions.

Ascertaining the view of the other is important in understanding human phenomena. African responses and actions,
however, have too often been examined from Eurocentric perspectives.[11] The misunderstandings between Europeans and
others have provoked in me an interest in alternative perspectives. What is attempted in these pages is a critical reevaluation of social phenomena on the basis of an Afrocentric
orientation.

A Place to Stand

The critic's chief problem is finding a place to stand—so to
speak—in relation to Western standards, imposed as interpretative measures on other cultures. I have familiarized myself with the leading proponents of the logic of scientific discovery, only to find their reductionist views of the world
incapable of adequately dealing with African cultural data. In
fact, it is questionable whether they are able to examine any
data that are dynamic and transformational. Since the time-
space domain is not stationary, and has not been considered
to be so since the Newtonian view was shattered by the quantum theory's evidence of particle-wave behavior, there needs
to be an accommodating, flexible frame of reference that per-
mits the dynamic.

A promising attempt to account for the harmony of op-
posites and break down the false dichotomies that occur in

much social science and physical science research is found in the work of Thomas Kuhn. It is promising as a heuristic, not as an accomplished end, because Kuhn does not question the ground upon which he stands. The procedure for scientific discovery, in Kuhn's view, is two-dimensional, including verifiability and falsifiability.[12] However, the Kuhnian paradigm has been considered a copy of Karl Popper's logic of discovery. Kuhn pointed out the similarities and differences between his views and Popper's in a rather lengthy paper[13] that accounts for differentiating between the logic of discovery and the psychology of research. Although he admits that he and Popper selected the same scientific aspects to investigate, he says they differ in how they perceive these aspects and in how they evaluate their significance. The areas of agreement are (1) scientific development is a dynamic process; (2) science is not accretion of concepts; it is, rather, a transformation of conceptual frames; (3) history often provides facts; and (4) outstanding science should be viewed as revolution. However, Kuhn argues, they arrive at these conclusions by different analytical modes.

Both Kuhn and Popper are primarily concerned with falsification and verification. While Popper believes that scientific revolutions occur when there is falsification of a theory, Kuhn argues for the joint approach of verification and falsification. The progress of science is supposed to occur when the crises of revolution are resolved. In my view, both the Kuhnian and the Popperian arguments, while certainly powerful within the context of European science, fail to raise the first-order question, which asks for a justification of the scientific endeavor itself. Rather than discuss the relative differences between revolutionary and normal science, one might question the scientific perspective itself or, as Stephen Toulmin did, the notion of revolutionary when used in connection with science. Yet it is clear that Kuhn has introduced a controversial and creative idea, despite the fact that he must, as he says of scientists, defend his own commitments while assuming a universal role. He cannot question the ground he stands on. It is essentially a materialist view.

The materialistic view of reality seems to have its roots in Greek philosophy. Aristotle (384 B.C.–322 B.C.), who is sometimes described, by Westerners, as "the master of all who know,"[14] defines the soul as the function of the body and argues that body functions are the individual's behaviors that are observable and should be, therefore, measurable. This is a stance that articulates the empirical trend in Greek philosophy. The inductive approach for collecting data and, later, verifying it by the logical, deductive approach is a major contribution of Aristotle. Aristotle's view of humans is, in the final analysis, a reductionist, deterministic, operationist positivistic view that motivated the modern behavioristic school to call for real science, free from mentalistic concepts and subjective methods.

I consider Aristotle a reductionist because he views behavior as a function of the body and assumes that nothing goes beyond what the organism does. He views the psychological functions in relation to physiological mechanisms. He is deterministic because he assumes that everything that happens in the universe can be accounted for by definite laws of causation. His view assumes that human behavior is subject to natural laws and must, therefore, be explained in terms of causative factors within the individual's heredity and environment. Aristotle is an operationist since he instructs the scientist to check the validity of his findings by examining the validity of the operations used in arriving at these findings. He is a positivist since he assumes that the goal of the scientist is to verify a hypothesis by searching for a natural principle as it exists in nature.

Fundamental to the materialist idea is the separation of mind-body. From the seventeenth to the nineteenth century, philosophers assimilated new information of scientific discovery in physics, chemistry, and biology and, accordingly, sharpened their philosophical views to articulate new views on human nature. The question of the mind-body dichotomy persists in the literature of Western philosophy to the present day. The psychologist Quill points out:

> In considering the body-mind problem, one embarks upon a tradition of inquiry which many have undertaken during the long history of philosophical thought—however, the whole issue of mind and body has been periodically discredited as a pseudo-problem and hence repressed. This latter attitude has been predominant during the last forty years, particularly in positivistically oriented "philosophies" and "psychologies." One of the increasing number of current testimonies to the fact that [the] mind-body problem is still highly problematic is that the Minnesota Center for Philosophy of Science devoted an entire volume, entitled Concepts, Theories, and the Mind-Body Problem, to studying the issue. . . . Obviously men of great ability—men who formerly regarded the mind-body problem as a pseudo-issue—in response to valid criticism, now find the problem to be a genuinely substantive one.[15]

For whom is it a genuine problem? The Afrocentric writer knows that oppositional dichotomies in real, everyday experiences do not exist. The speaker or the writer is fully engaged in every way, not merely in ways that seem measurable. You may use the word *processor*, but you cannot understand all that is involved in my writing by observing my fingers. I may experience hunger, joy, pain, or pleasure while I write. I might even get an electric shock or two, but you would not know that from observation, unless I shrieked. I might experience the most delightful romantic thoughts while I strike the keyboard to produce unromantic prose. This flow of energy cannot be accounted for by mere observation of the physical movements of the writer as he writes, nor of the report of what he describes in his writings, nor even to what he testifies has crossed his mind as he is writing. The interaction of his physical and metaphysical world leads to his behavior at the moment, and this interaction cannot be reduced to separate units of an either/or nature of body-mind. It cannot be assumed that the body causes the mental activities, or that mental activities cause the body to function. Accounting for different perspectives or allowing them to emerge becomes the principal aim of a truly liberating perspective.

While the contributions of the Eurocentric philosophers and scientists have been important and valuable, they have not been fully expressive of the extent or power of human ways of knowing. The arguments that have been advanced for the Western formulation of science are not convincing. Marvin Harris, for example, writes as good an *apologia* as anyone for the values of science:

> Science is a unique and precious contribution of western civilization. . . . No other way of knowing is based on a set of rules explicitly designed to transcend the prior belief systems of mutually antagonistic tribes, nations, classes, and ethnic and religious communities in order to arrive at knowledge that is equally probable for any rational human mind. . . . The real alternative to science is not anarchy, but ideology; not peaceful artists, philosophers and anthropologists, but aggressive fanatics and messiahs, eager to annihilate each other and the world if need be in order to prove their point.[16]

Harris characterizes the scientific story as superior to other cultures and claims it to be uniquely rational among systems. Harris is perhaps at his Eurocentric best as an interpreter of the nonscientists of other cultures. He readily admits that there are "domains of experience the knowledge of which cannot be achieved by adherence to the rules of scientific method."[17] But he sees this "nonscientific" knowledge as beyond his understanding, particularly "the ecstatic knowledge of mystics and saints; the visions and hallucinations of drug users and of schizophrenics; and the aesthetic and moral insights of artists, poets, and musicians."[18] This is almost fantastic: an admission that he cannot distinguish between the euphoria of drug users and saints or schizophrenics and the insights of artists and poets!

Harris's characterization of the Western scientific method is by no means unique. Yet his ability to denigrate other ways of knowing creates a false impression of science itself. Science does not exclude moral or aesthetic insight. The special disciplines and rigors of the arts and the regularized, methodical procedures of the so-called mystics cannot be easily discounted. Artistic contributions and so-called mystical achievements have added knowledge and richness to the human experience.

What Harris and other apologists of the peculiarly narrow version of the scientific adventure argue against is what they perceive as the random, mystical type of discovery. They see it as valuable only when it is transformed into precise, logical verification. Thus discovery is separate from verification. In effect, Harris's view would dismiss the creative process, divest itself of discovery, and concentrate on the verification process. My desire is to see a paradigm of complementarity that integrates discovery with verification where necessary. In this manner, Afrocentricity expands the repertoire of human perspectives on knowledge.

The Afrocentric View

The term *Afrology,* coined in *Afrocentricity: The Theory of Social Change,* denotes the Afrocentric study of African concepts, issues, and behaviors.[19] It includes research on African themes in the Americas and the West Indies, as well as the African continent. Most of the relevant research involves the systematic exploration of relationships, social codes, cultural and commercial customs, and oral traditions and proverbs, although interpretation of communicative behaviors, as expressed in discourse, spoken or written, and techniques found in jazz studies and urban street-vernacular signifying, is also included. Human beings tend to recognize three fundamental existential postures one can take with respect to the human condition: feeling, knowing, and acting. Afrology recognizes these three stances as interrelated, not separate. Europeans normally call these categories *affective, cognitive,* and *conative.* The affective component deals with a person's feelings, of liking or disliking, about an object or idea. The cognitive refers to how an object is perceived, its conceptual connotation. Conative is the person's behavioral tendencies regarding an object. However, in Afrology, the study of an object or idea is best performed when all three components are interrelated. This present book, therefore, is an Afrological undertaking as much as anything else.

Perhaps the most important theoretical impetus to this line of study came from the earlier theorizing of Wade Nobles, Maulana Karenga, and Leachem Semaj. In his works, Nobles is primarily preoccupied with psychological states and conditions of an oppressed people. Karenga and Semaj are interested mainly in developing theories of cultural reconstruction. They argue that diasporic Africans are often disconnected from positive African values. Thus the need for reconstruction. Their work contributes to the overall Afrological enterprise.

What I have done is bring the consciousness of rhetorical structure to the study of African communication, particularly discourse. I will try to set a conceptual field for exploring the Afrocentric perspective on discourse. In doing this, I will explain the rhetorical condition as a phenomenon with an implicit structure and establish the position of a metatheory for African communication. I examine African American oratory as the totalization of the Afrocentric perspective, emphasizing the presence of *nommo* in African discourse and in specific instances of resistance to the dominant ideology. In the oratorical experience, much as in the jazz experience, the African person finds the ability to construct a discourse reality capable of calling forth *nommo,* the generative and productive power of the spoken word. The idea of this book is to propose what an Afrocentric theory might examine and to perform an interpretation of discourse based on Afrocentric values where *nommo* as word-force is a central concept.

I will rely to some extent on the work of Burgest, who has argued that there are *afro-circular* and *euro-linear* values at work in social relations between blacks and whites in America.[20] This view is similar to the position I advanced in intercultural communication theory regarding the Afrocentric-personalism, Asiocentric-spiritualism, and Eurocentric-materialism categories of reality. Burgest's concepts are useful when I want to identify the essence of the two principal views, although I do not agree with Burgest on all details of what constitutes afro-circularity and euro-linearity. (He considers these two views the only ones of significance, including Asian with African as *Eastern*, and calls the European view *Western*. We know now that if there is an alliance of views, it is European and Asian combined, for a Eurasian view, and another called an African view.) Nevertheless, the terms *afro-circular* and *euro-linear* adequately express my conception of the views of Africans and Eurasians. One can see the emerging outlines of the constraints of an afro-circular view within the euro-linear definition by examining almost any genre of Western thought.

In the succeeding pages, I shall show how rhetoric in the euro-linear world is controlled by the structural conditions inherent in the process. The point is that a euro-linear view seeks to predict and to control. An afro-circular view seeks to interpret and understand. These are different human objectives, derived from historical and cultural experiences. What occurs in any science or art, such as rhetoric, is a debate over mode, over structure, over condition—that is, the guidelines for what constitutes the valid discussion of discourse. On a larger scale, the topic is a conversation about the plurality of vision in the context of reality.

We all have the capacity to see, and usually this is from the vantage point of our culture. In the West and elsewhere, the European has propounded an exclusive view of reality that creates a fundamental human crisis. In some cases it has created cultures arrayed against themselves.

Part 1   **The Situation**

Attempts to understand African
American "orature" have failed because
they misconstrue the nature and
character of African American
discourse, written or spoken. Often
ignorant of African philosophy and
culture, commentators have imposed
Western constructs and values on
material that grows out of coherent,
albeit different, traditions. The result
has been a failure to understand or
value that material, as well as an
inability to recognize or correct that
failure. Orature represents the total
body of oral discourses, styles, and
traditions of African people. Only when
we examine orature as we have studied
literature can we construe the totality of
African culture.

Rhetorical Condition as a Conceptual Field

Einstein is quoted as having said modern quantum physics "is theory which decides what we can observe."[1] What Einstein meant was that the scientist's freedom is restricted by the language he accepts. It is impossible to break out of a narrow frame of reference if you are not given the capability to dream of what can be. Only certain kinds of information can be acquired if we employ certain kinds of theoretical rules. Noam Chomsky found this in language and Howard Gardner (of Project Zero) has indicated as much in the patterns of music. However, the linguistic and cognitive patterns are not the only generators of restriction; one can be restricted by the general political situation, where the rules of the game are different for different players.

The last five hundred years of world history have been devastating for the acquisition of knowledge about other than European cultures. Dominated by whites in Asia, Africa, and Latin America, victimized people have expressed their desire to redress their grievances. Paulo Freire has said (in *The Politics of Education*)[2] that true education is a liberating experience for the peasant. Beyond this, however, is the fact that certain political constructs impose definite limitations in concepts and content on all discourse about reality. Out of these limitations the oppressed, non-free people, who are exploited by ruling classes, those whose wills are enforced, are challenged to struggle against structural discourse that denies their right to freedom and, indeed, their right to existence. Ultimately, the acting out or the speaking out of the word is also confined to the categories established by the early power brokers for the dominant society. That is why I speak of the empowering of the oppressed by listening to their voices.

Rhetorical Conditions and Power Structures

Rhetoric has been tied to the linguistic postulate that the form of a public discourse must express a statement that is reasonably controlled by the emitter, and one that can potentially be understood by the receiver. This is a euro-linear construction, situated in a stimulus-response ideology, that places responsibility on both the sender and the receiver of a message's content and expression. This view explicates form in the common sense of order of sentence structure—in effect, the syntactical dimension. Yet as far as the African American communicator is concerned, perhaps the most authentic, overarching symbol in discourse is the structure of the rhetorical condition itself. Structure becomes a form of discourse, apart from its character, in the words of a discourse.

Rhetorical condition is the structure and power pattern, assumed or imposed, during a rhetorical situation by society. Although the condition may be negotiated by the communicators, different rhetorical situations produce different conditions because the inherent power relationships change from situation to situation. I do not mean traditional structural concerns of discourse, that is, arrangement and style; these follow almost naturally from the structure of the *discourse as discourse*. There is a rhetoric of structure, not in the sense of a rhetoric about structure, but rather a rhetoric of form about the rhetoric of words. While the structure affects all users of language, it functions to maintain white supremacist views in a rhetorical—that is, symbolic—as well as a political sense.

Structure constitutes a parallel message to the internal structure of discourse. Although Rosenthal was astute in his observations about corollary symbols, he never considered structure itself.[3] Bitzer, on the other hand, wanted to know the context out of which a speaker or writer created discourse.[4] Thus, Lloyd Bitzer is clear, the rhetorical situation is a natural context of persons, events, objects, relations, and an exigence that evokes an utterance. Both Paul Rosenthal and Lloyd Bitzer are ultimately interested in the context of discourse, yet neither recognizes the inherent structural constraints on the context.

Ordinary language philosophers such as Austin and Searle, unlike Rosenthal and Bitzer, have started from the concept of structure in detail, particularly as it relates to the postulates of philosophical reasoning.[5] They have provided some challenging concepts in grammatical usage, but their view is limited for our understanding of the large structural characteristics of a rhetorical condition. Interest in types of propositions may tell us something about the philosopher's linguistic inclinations but it does not get us closer to the question of the overarching condition of discourse in the African American or African context. One might discover, say, that in authoritarian discourse the imperative form is an obvious power set-up in a communicative situation. And we might admit that the use of an imperative in a rhetorical discourse establishes a social environment that signals power. But ultimately the structure of the rhetorical condition is chosen first. Those who listen to a discourse may choose to accept or to resist the structural form of the discourse, yet the choosing of the form—for example, *forensic, deliberate, ceremonial, sermonic,* or *agitational*—is itself the initial commitment to a certain outcome because the rhetorical condition is established as soon as the form is chosen. Madhubuti has said that the black American leaders tend to choose the sermonic form, which limits them in the arena of power. White leaders tend to emerge from business, the academy, and the professions, but blacks, because of the word, tend to find their leaders in the pulpit.[6]

The shortcomings of the sermonic form as a means to power

are the least of our worries in the world of ideas. More importantly, the sermon itself is a captive of a larger, more politically significant context. Sermons exist within the framework of the political or ideological context in which the speaker exists. As such, the sermon as a discourse form pays homage to a meta-form of discourse that directs the details of what is possible at any given moment in the sermon. An imperialism of framework operates as viciously as any political or intellectual imperialism ever operated. There is, in the final analysis, a profound dilemma in discourse that articulates itself in the way we, as humans, choose to handle the structural condition. Rhetorical condition, therefore, is not an illusionary concept; it is the source of the subtle machinations of power and manipulation of words and lesser forms.

But how are we to understand discourse in this society, given the rhetorical condition? Daudi provides a significant insight into its nature when he contends that discourse "is the object of a struggle for power."[7] So the real question is "not what is said but who says? And why does he say so? Who takes possession of the discourse, and for what purpose does he do it?"[8] Daudi's point seems to be the importance of power in discourse. Who takes possession of the word? What use is made of the discourse? So now we must ask further, What constitutes a rhetoric of structure? How does one distinguish it from a rhetoric of words? Both are symbolic, yet a rhetoric of structure achieves its ends despite the modification of the stylistic elements of discourse so long as structure remains the same. For example, it does not matter if the language of the imperative is polite and gentle, so long as the imperative structure endures; a social environment has been created where one, for instance, gives orders and the other is expected to obey. Sometimes this occurs in social situations where political and economic power resides in one class or one race and powerlessness in another class or race, for example, South African whites and blacks. Such a rhetorical condition seldom allows reciprocity, despite the illusion, within the framework of a unidirectional perspective. Black communicators tend to seek a redress by moving to neutralize unidirectional rhetoric.

Take, for example, the power of a speaker in an imperative situation. Since the imperative mood in English normally finds its source in the indicative, which expresses a fact that is not in doubt, it becomes the task of the speaker to express that fact. However, whatever reality may exist in the future is held in abeyance by the speaker's attitude as he or she makes pertinent and prudent commands within the context of the rhetorical condition. The speaker, who therefore can control the future, controls a portion of time, and holds a key to the audience's knowledge. Thus, the imperative mood commands the listeners, directs their knowledge, and assesses their performance. An Afrocentric theory explains how one can disidentify from controlling structures, because it is so easy for structure to take over from content and manipulate the message, orchestrate it, at will. Although structure as discourse prevails in all rhetorical situations (Bitzerian), it is politics and religion that provide the more obvious examples. Goldschlager believes that the goal of both religion and politics is to win, not to convince reasonably.[9] He misunderstands the true purpose of rhetorical discourse and has little or no conception of black discourse, because he fails to see its operation in the practical world, that is, in the arena of human interactions in the give and take of decision making, one of the principal civilizing marks of our species.

The confirmation of our freedom and responsibility occurs in the decisions that we make. Therefore, both religion and politics, in the normal course of their activities, seek to win but seek to win reasonably, that is, in such a way as to be perceived as being reasonable. The fact that the reasons employed may not be good enough for the logician or the rhetorician who demands not merely a *perception of rationality* but rationality does not negate the fact that both the speaker and the audience in politics and religion assume credibility in their enterprise. However, the same discourse may be rejected by the audience as unconvincing in its reasons or reasoning.

Of course, when significant persons possess "special" knowledge that is unavailable to us, we are more willing to defer to the priests, rabbis, shamans, and preachers. And in our communities we are not devoid of charismatic preachers who use language to demonstrate their special calling. Marcus Garvey, Martin Luther King Jr., Malcolm X, Maulana Karenga, Louis Farrakhan, and Jesse Jackson are consummate orators in the historical tradition.

Since power finds its efficacy in acquiescence, messages structured in a hierarchical manner reduce the leverage of the audience to respond to an incomplete or fragmentary discourse. There are several discourse forms that are hierarchical in the sense they assume that certain communicators hold higher positions of rank, for example, *criticism, sermons, lectures.* Each of these forms, as examples, operating in the rhetorical situation, is structural in character, apart from structure in the message organization. Discourse forms, such as criticism or sermons, are pragmatic and efficient and as such they support the established order, whatever that order happens to be. Marcuse contends that the political system dictates the mode of discourse.[10] In his analysis of the present era, human beings are pretty much manipulated by the architectonic industrial-political-technical environment. What comes out of the speaker's mouth is determined by the society. At another level, however, rhetorical structure dictates relationships, whether in a Marxist or a capitalist society. Marcuse asserts that the immense productivity of the modern economic system provides and satisfies human wants while checking any speculation or emergence that might challenge the established order.

It is clear that any criticism, whether Marxist or capitalist, implies the ability of the critic to judge, assess, evaluate the other. The act of criticizing, therefore, is an act of imposition: One imposes one's own standards onto the other. In order for critical discourse to be effective and valuable, the recipient must acquiesce. In fact, the entire history of Africans in the United States has been marked by a singular resistance to criticism from those who have sought to deny civil and human rights to blacks. Furthermore, this resistance is one supreme negation of the imposition of a racist and oppressive discourse. Nevertheless, the wielding of critical power confers authority in the practical arena of discourse, whether in legislative bodies, political meetings, or intellectual gatherings. It cannot do otherwise, because its natural form is autoreferential. The black politician who criticizes the political policies of the opposition sets herself or himself up as an authority capable of assessing the other. And while the challenge to the opposition is always cast in a hierarchical form, it is not necessarily sustained in the face of a counterchallenge.

Characteristics of Hierarchical Discourse

There are three characteristics for a condition of hierarchical discourse: control over the rhetorical territory through definition, establishment of a self-perpetuating initiation or *rite de passage*, and the stifling of opposing discourse. These characteristics may be seen in the rhetoric of domination. One way to create ambiguity is to redefine established terms in such a manner that the original meaning is lost. Wherever ambiguity exists, the established order is able to occupy the ground of clarity by contending that ambiguity did not exist prior to the rise of the opposition, although the established order may have participated in creating the ambiguous situation. In this manner, the established order can undercut the opposition and manipulate the pattern of communication for its own effect. By defining not only the terms of discussion but also the grounds upon which the discussion will be waged, the established order concentrates power in its own hands.

Octavio Paz has contended that the established order has the ability to impose one vision of the world while exterminating another vision.[11] This is a power unknown to the victims—as victims. It is reserved for the established order by will or power. Thus when one says—as Jerry Falwell, the

American leader of the Moral Majority, said after a visit to South Africa in 1985—that the Western world should not impose democracy on the South Africans, one misunderstands the nature of the established order, the Nationalist government of Pieter Botha. No one can impose democracy from the outside; however, the government can prevent democracy from occurring from within by essentially preventing people from choosing it. This is the way the discourse of condition, of structure, operates to confound the best reasons of the victims; it prevents choice. And the prevention of choice is fundamentally an intellectual terrorism, carried on by the established order opposed to the liberation of Freire's peasant. Therefore, the imposition of one vision and the extermination of others must be confronted on intellectual grounds.

The second characteristic of hierarchical discourse is that it creates a self-perpetuating ritual whereby the truth, in effect, is reserved for those who are initiated. To be initiated, in this context, would mean to adhere to a given position. The votarists of a particular position will have received the "word" from some certifying authority. I am not suggesting that audiences are by definition not a part of the initiated; there are too many contrary examples where those defined as audients stand on the floor and speak to their fellows in a manner that sets up the structural pattern. Apart from whether or not the speaker from the floor supports the established order, the speaker, by virtue of *taking* the floor, participates in a hierarchical situation that provides its own message. Furthermore, it is a situation within a larger "fixed" situation where the rules are set, often against the interests of the new speaker.

There are several ways in which one may take the floor: One may raise a hand to "acquire" the floor; one may proceed to the front of an audience to speak; or one may shout a message from a position in the audience, without being recognized. Initially, such a person is assumed to have something to say, although, after listening, the audience might accept or reject the speaker's message. Nevertheless, the seizing of the ground is itself an act of assertion, and by that act the speaker establishes a hierarchical structure that mirrors the established order, although the message content may be different from what it would be if it emanated from established leaders.

On the other hand, all institutions, whether public or private, are fluid in their leadership structure and policies, and what may parade as the established order today may not be so tomorrow. Audiences have been known to shout speakers down as an attempt to strip them of power. The assumption of the floor is no guarantee of the permanence of structural advantage. Those who speak from the floor today, to criticize the established order, may indeed be the ones who are criticized tomorrow. This is true, even though a skillful rhetor may maneuver an audience by manipulating the rhetorical structure. A speaker whose rhetorical forte is counterargument may want to engage the audience in debate, thereby turning the structure to advantage.

The third characteristic of hierarchical discourse is the stifling of opposing discourse. Since no power position is permanent and all institutions seek to perpetuate themselves, institutions often choose to denounce all opposing views, through direct confrontation (as on a battlefield), through subterfuge (as in indirect attacks on the opposition's character or in the trenches of dialectical combat), or in giving the opposing view the illusion of a channel of expression (which is, in reality, controlled by the established order). Since only the votarists are uniquely qualified to expatiate on a given subject, the opposition's words are not to be taken seriously. This is the position that is assumed by those who occupy the summit of the established pyramid. At this rarefied height, knowledge increases, and the numbers decrease. Those who would oppose come from the broad base of the pyramid and consequently are devoid of the symbol of power, which is reserved only for those who have knowledge. Yet, the act of speaking to a group as opposition momentarily re-orders the structure of power.

To have the floor is valuable as a structural symbol of power, regardless of how briefly one holds the floor. To stifle the opposition, therefore, those in positions of power seek to keep the opposition away from every idiom of power. Thus, an individual who seeks to challenge authority will find that not only are the facts often inaccessible, but it is likely that the access to a message channel and access to a formal discourse situation are also unavailable. The established order prevails by demonstrating, in its absolute occupation of the symbolic and structural ground, that the opposition does not exist. Invisibility is the ultimate defense—out of sight, out of mind. It appears to the opposition that a tyranny of occupation sits astride its attempt to achieve equity. Thus the Afrocentric psychologist, Akbar, contends that intellectual oppression involves the use of abusive language, ideas, and concepts to degrade a people.[12] In reality, the entire social fabric of oppression is dictated by symbols of hierarchy and intellectual theories rooted in Eurocentric viewpoints.

More importantly, many blacks and most whites do not see that the symbols are dominated by European values, which creates "new speaker" or "different speaker" categories.

Hierarchical discourse operates in ideological contexts. But that is perhaps not to say much, since all discourse is contextual, and context is defined ideologically in most cases. However, what we mean is that hierarchical discourse that seeks to maintain its hierarchical position is supported by ideology. Without the ideological context, the discourse is vacuous, a hollow form without power. Given a context, the discourse assumes an awesome power as supporter of an entire worldview whose material base may be rooted in history. The more authoritarian these contexts, the more rigid the discourse structure.

This point can be clarified by examining hierarchical discourse in relationship to the common stimulus-response, sender-receiver, speaker-audience model. The paradigm itself hinges on hierarchy and a formidable structure is proposed that dictates the relationship between the message sender and receiver. This structure, I contend, is inherently unequal and constitutes an inequity that in one way mirrors cultural expansion. Daudi is clear on this issue when he says, "What we today call reason and rationalism have no intrinsic value. Our concept of reason was founded in relation to its exterior, in what reason defined as its opposite. Our culture, as its fundamental element, suddenly reveals itself to be founded on its margins."[13]

Daudi is, of course, stating an empirical view. While he condemns reason as the principal source of knowledge, thereby challenging the rationalist position, he enthrones empiricism. Neither rationalism nor empiricism encompasses all the ways of knowing; certainly the existential and so-called mystical ways of knowing constitute varieties of human knowing. Suffice it to say, at the moment, that when the sender-receiver model is adhered to, it is by nature one in which a tutor and a tutoree participate. What is potentially detrimental in that situation is the power-dependency formula that exists in so much discourse. To question the tutor, to challenge the sender, must remain a part of any liberating discourse.

At least two methods of discourse are open to the receiver in opposition to the speaking power. Both methods are based in the nature of the authority exercised over the structure by the speaking power. Since the ruling power tries to impose silence by presenting an "undebatable word," the receiver must present the most debatable symbol. This is why a culture that would refuse to exploit occupies a different ground than the exploiting culture. The second method of attack is the use of guerrilla rhetoric, the multifrontal verbal attacks on the structural symbol of the speaking power itself. To concentrate only on the words would be to allow the authoritarian discourse structure to continue as unassailable because of its superior ground position in determining how the battle should be waged. That is precisely why black students of the 1960s who successfully agitated for the establishment of Afro-American Studies departments had to resort to "nonnegotiable demands." Negotiation is the ground of the speaking power, the sender of the S–R model; consequently, students, and particularly black students, would be in an unequal position to negotiate with university administrators. In a larger sense, the receiver must attack the architectonics of authoritarian discourse, showing it to be an artificial structure. Most audiences are bound to linguistic and formal structures, not to content; and the ruling powers will seek to use parades, the flag, the star, torchlights, the swastika, the monkeytail swatter of the late Jomo Kenyatta, the cross, or the Ku Klux Klan hood as signs of omniscience.[14] The receiver who employs a substitute discourse or guerrilla rhetoric successfully against the voice of force, so that the voice itself falls silent, must guard against the inevitable temptation to employ the same discourse tactics as the fallen force.

A history of black protest in America and recently in South Africa has shown that the power that inheres in the rhetorical condition by virtue of its established position can be effectively challenged if the intended receivers of the message reject the message. Of course, this is asking that consciousness be elevated to the point where the receivers-victims know what is happening to them. There cannot be any effective power unless the victims of rhetorical dictatorship, by force or acquiescence, allow it to continue. Revolt—intellectual, moral, or rhetorical—is a sign of rejection. Daudi says, "All knowledge is political, not because it may have political consequences or be politically useful, but because knowledge has its conditions of possibility in power relations."[15] The rhetorical condition is symbolic of the political structure; it thrives on the same principles and it liberates or imprisons its interactants on the same philosophical grounds. Power relations create politics and politics creates, *inter alia*, power relations.

In establishing this perspective, you can see that I am proposing not only a new perspective but a different framework for understanding human behavior. A people who have been relegated to the fringes of the society must now be looked upon as players in the field, albeit players who have operated from a position of less power for the past four hundred years. Only an ample metatheory can adequately consider the multidimensions of the black communicative experience; and this metatheory is founded on Afrocentric bases.

The necessity of this world of thought can be seen by a simple analysis of the European philosophical outlook since Plato and Aristotle. Lovejoy's position is stated clearly when he writes (in *The Great Chain of Being*) that "the most fundamental of the group of ideas of which we are to review the history appears first in Plato; and nearly all that follows might therefore serve as an illustration of a celebrated remark of Professor Whitehead's, that 'the safest general characterization of the European philosophical tradition is that it consists of a series of footnotes to Plato.'"[16]

Unfortunately, these footnotes to Plato become central arguments in the European reach for intellectual exclusivity. All roads backwards supposedly lead to the Greeks, regardless of the discipline or field of study. I recall reading an essay on technology in which Daniel Bell argued that "the contemplative tradition of mind" goes back to Greece.[17] If one shows an interest in drama, the Eurocentric author points this person to Sophocles' comedies and tragedies; in art, to the perfection of Greek sculpture; in history, to Herodotus and Thucydides; in epic poetry, to Homer; in rhetoric, to Aristotle's *Rhetoric* and Plato's *Phaedrus* and *Gorgias—ad infinitum*, it seems. With this line of thinking and no intellectual correctives, the scholar will assume that no other universe of thought exists; and, in fact, it is impossible to conceive of another universe of thought so long as one is ensconced in this intellectual cocoon. Thus Ibn Battuta, who probably travelled as far and wide as Marco Polo (with as much significance) within the same general time frame, is hardly known by educated Westerners. Clever Aphrodite, as she had done with Narcissus because of his obstinacy, allows Eurocentric writers to see their own reflections and to fall violently in love with what they see.

So overwhelming is the impact of Greco-Roman traditions that almost every American student knows the Colosseum or Parthenon before he or she knows the Empire State Building, the Tiber before the Mississippi, and Aristotle before Du Bois. The "glory that was Greece" and "grandeur that was Rome" completely blinded the subsequent interpreters of the achievements of those cultures; but even worse, so handicapped the

northern and western European thinkers that they could not
see that Greece and Rome had more in common with Africa
than, say, Scandinavia.

The academy is not yet fully alive to the important transformation being brought about by the developing African world
consciousness. It is always difficult to recognize decisive steps
in theoretical development when one is in immediate prox-
imity and the steps are so gradual. Sustained by new information and innovative methodologies, Afrology will transform
community and social sciences, as well as arts and humanities,
and assist in constructing a new, perhaps more engaging, way
to analyze and synthesize reality. Perhaps what is needed is a
post-Western or meta-Western metatheory to disentangle us
from the consuming monopoly of a limited intellectual framework, but first let us establish the idea of an Afrocentric
metatheory.

The Idea of a Metatheory

A metatheory suggests the character and content of theories
in the sense that it prescribes what a theory should explain
(how African American language developed, or how it is used
in urban communities, or what is its essence) and what analytical methodologies are required for revealing and establishing concepts such as symbolic engineering and expressive
artifact. A metatheory, then, is the product of decision rather
than discovery, and it is justified by the theories that are consonant to it.

The process of discovering "natural laws" is instructive,
and discovery is based on observable phenomena. When observations seem to lead to the same generalization, the scientist says a law exists. Once the law is contradicted by new observations that lead to another generalization, it ceases being
a natural law. As Steinmann understood, "without meta-
research, there can be no investigation of any phenomenon."[18]

Ebonics, for example, could only find a theoretical base because of metagrammatical research. The prototypical language of African Americans has been named *Ebonics* in order to distinguish it from English. The word is a composite of *ebony* and *phonetics.*

Rhetoric, in an Afrocentric sense, is the productive thrust of language into the unknown in an attempt to create harmony and balance in the midst of disharmony and indecision. The uses of rhetoric are varied, and it is necessary to include the production of disharmony in its utility. The presence of counteracting rhetorics sets up tensions that often thrust one rhetoric in the role of creating disharmony. Language itself compounds the problems of the unknown, for it is being made as the speaker speaks. That is why it is possible to say that the black speaker, or any speaker who senses the nature of words as artifacts, glimpses the limits of rhetoric. In this sense, rhetoric is not a science; it is an art. That is to say, a certain inventive skill is needed in managing words and sentences to be effective as a communicator.

An inventional scheme for African communication behavior will have possible implications for a more general theory. Such a frame, in its metatheoretical dimensions, must be adequately broad to accommodate diverse and conflicting approaches to the generation of innovations. Every use of language is unlike any other; and some uses might even be contextually paradoxical. Adequacy of metatheory, therefore, is defined not by a single theoretical statement, but by its allowance for the self-aggrandizement of any theory. In this sense the metatheory becomes architectonic as an organizing scheme by which all else is explained. Such a metatheory must be inclusive in order to account for the prototypical language styles and myths of the culture. Beyond that, it must explain the peculiar social focus of black language in America and, by that explanation, become interpretative of symbolic engineering in a multiethnic situation. Accordingly, social or political change is nothing more than the transmitting of information as an act of power in this scheme.

As an inclusive plan, this metatheory, for example, places

William Labov and Walt Wolfram's structural works in the same communication family as William Stewart's historical analysis of black language behavior.[19] This much is clear and surely reflective of traditional associative patterns along disciplinary lines. Even clearer, however, is the fact that Thomas Kochman's ethnography of black street language and the descriptive work on black spoken discourse, called *ethno-rhetoric*, belongs to the same inclusive plan.

This perspective employs ideas from numerous social scientists and humanists, particularly those who call themselves Afrologists, and regards them as pilots to comprehension of African American language and cultural behavior. Such a perspective begins with a linguistic foundation, in the sense of an explication of structure, and moves towards an understanding of the symbolisms employed in practical discourse. The path from one point to the other is tedious, but it is this process that must be explained if we are ever to know anything substantial about how African Americans use language and behave in public and private.

Practicable theories are developed on the basis of plausible, coherent principles that explain certain phenomena; so, clearly, one function of a metatheory would be to accommodate principles for the explanation of theoretical phenomena related to African American communication. The various social class constructs, language deficit models, and case histories, as well as surrealistic rhetoric and the lyrical quality of black discourse style, can be successfully conceptualized within the framework of the metatheory.[20]

The constituents of the metatheory are *frame of mind, scope of context, structure of code,* and *delivery of message.* This fundamental analytical system allows us to be open to the infinite potentialities of communication, and the constituents of this metatheory aid us in determining the innovations in African American communicative behavior without an undue concentration on either grammatical, syntactical, semantic, or lexical components.

The significance of any metatheory is that it not only explains a given cluster of theories but also provides opportunity for enlarging human understanding generally. It is now possible to explore the relationship among the constituents as they help to interpret the sweep of black language and discourse patterns within the context of the American society.

A metatheory is no more valid than the theories that are consonant to it; or more exactly, those theories justify the metatheory. Insofar as I have chosen the metatheory on the basis of the theories, the metatheory has been decided upon in terms of the character of the theories. For example, the claim by linguisticians that even when specific vocabularies are no longer employed, the phonological and morphological patterns of certain groups of African Americans reflect an African past, is consistent with the metatheoretical constituents. Yet also true is Henry Mitchell's contention that the prevailing rhetorical quality of the black preacher is lyrical. Mitchell argues that the black preacher is even required to use the black intonation and accent, because "no black man can truly identify with a God who speaks only the language of the white oppressor."[21]

Rhythm, Styling, and Sound

It would be nonsense to argue that theories which emerge about black language and discourse can claim uniformity in black behavior; but the variance among blacks is less than between blacks and non-blacks.[22] Dixon and Foster state that six essential elements comprise the black referent: (1) the value of humanism, (2) the value of communalism, (3) the attribute of oppression/paranoia, (4) the value of empathetic understanding, (5) the value of rhythm, and (6) the principle of limited reward.[23] There is, in addition, a seventh element: the principle of styling. So in writing about the frame of mind I am emphasizing how certain social, creative, and psychological factors contribute to a total view of language. In isolating any part of this language for linguistic or rhetorical studies (I mean at the simplest level, structural or persuasive), the frame of mind of the language user is important for analytical consideration. I know, for instance, that to the African American preacher, speaking in the proper frame of mind, "Jesus is my subject" is not the same as saying "Jee-sas is my subject." Baraka has made a similar observation regarding the singing of the song "Just a Closer Walk with Thee" and the way one changes the word *yeh* by moving the tongue.[24]

It is not my intention to discuss each of these elements; rather, I will concentrate on two elements that are more obviously related to the matter of language and rhetoric. The concepts of *rhythm* and *styling* seem indicative, in terms of our discussion, of the frame of mind. Rhythm in spoken discourse is a basic measure of the successful speech. How well a speaker can regulate his flow of words with the proper pauses of audience "indentations" becomes the standard for the black speaker before a basically black audience. Henry Mitchell refers to this as establishing "a kind of intimate fellowship." Sound periodicity dictates the communicative terms of black language. The effective users of the language recognize, almost naturally, the need to employ some form of rhythm in vocal expression. Usually the speaker employs the characteristic style of his audience so that his cadences are familiar to his hearers. Martin Luther King utilized the spoken language of his followers and the "sounding good" quality, frequently noted by observers, contributed to his success. A basic element in *sounding good* is to know when *not* to sound. The rhetorical pause used so brilliantly by Malcolm X in his speeches is an essential factor in the black frame of mind as it relates to rhythm in language. And as we shall see, rhythm is also the basis of African American transcendence.[25]

The regular clustering of tones according to accent and time value explains only a portion of the rhythmic frame of mind. Mitchell has observed that the African American style is dependent upon the audience's permissiveness. Most audiences (if allowed to be) are definers of communicative boundaries. They establish the limits of the speaker's effectiveness by their behaviors. To "keep" the audience, a speaker must *style*, and a key element of style is rhythm created by tone, accent, and meaning. Thus *to style* is an action, and when one styles one is engaged in creating a relationship.[26]

Styling refers to the conscious or unconscious manipulation of language or mannerisms to influence favorably the hearers of a message. A variety of behaviors is permitted to achieve the desired end. They may be classified according to the receiver's principal way of responding: visual and audio. Visual styling is effected by gestural or symbolic mannerisms. While the most common type of gesture in communication is purposive movement for meaning and emphasis, conscious styling movement is highly regarded by black speakers and hearers. Conventional gesticulation is concerned with description and emphasis, as in "The fish was *this* size" or "The point is well made that . . ."

Symbolic mannerisms, such as Martin Luther King Jr. touching the small upper pocket on his coat, are also a matter of visual styling. This gesture lends presence to the speaker who, in taking this liberty, shows the audience that he is not an average speaker but someone capable of handling his platform tasks with ease. Every speaker is not gifted with ability to employ unconventional gestures during a speech. A certain amount of verbal skill accompanies the speaker who uses visual styling. Other forms of visual styling are environmental, in the sense that they are connected to the principal constituents of a rhetorical situation (speaker, message, and receivers), but are primarily effected by the arrangement of physical surroundings or the sartorial habits of the speaker or his friends (e.g., in the '60s we saw the black leather jackets of Bobby Seale's guards, dashiki-clad youths on the platform behind Maulana Karenga, etc.). The genius of the speaker determines the quality of the visual styling. Of course, writers have no such cadre of visual symbols; speech is much more a collective experience than writing. Metaphors must gather the soldiers for writers.

What people hear in a speech is what rhetorical critics chiefly evaluate. Because of this, the response to African American vocal cues is significant. These cues may take several forms, including variations of pronunciation, intercalations, and malapropisms. Words are frequently intoned to give them a "soulful" quality. In an education meeting at a university, where a young speaker gave his view of education, he began by saying "Education is for the c-o-m-m-u-n-i-t-y. I mean commu-ni-ty." He was styling, and every person familiar with the "tradition" knew that the speaker had seized upon this stylistic device to have an impact. Between the speaker and the audience was an authentic bond, created by the spoken word.

Intercalations are the "filler" expressions that often appear as deliberate attempts at styling but become habitual with repeated use. In this category are "you know," "lookit," and "hey," which often find their way into the language mainstream. To be "cool" is to be capable of handling the verbal styling necessary to establish presence. Whereas rhythm and styling are major contributive factors in the African American speaker's frame of mind as it relates to language, the intercalations manifest in styling are interrelated to rhythm as a recurring sound or polyrhythms.[27] Historically, the expression "she sounded on him" underscored the importance of verbal expression. Although *sounding* carries the idea of verbal games, it is a precise description of both the rhythm and wit employed in language. Without rhythm or wit, one cannot "sound," since "sounding" is itself style.

The Context for Symbol Development

A second constituent in a metatheory would be the contextual scope of black language and rhetoric; it provides a basis for understanding how symbols are engineered. What are the social realities governing the development of black language? And what are the constraints upon black speakers against creating new rhetorics? The context must be comprised of the historical as well as the present moment in terms of resources for bringing about new language styles. One can describe the coming to be of a new object or event, whether new words or innovative phrases (or the "dozens"), by considering the creation in the light of these questions. What resources are available to the African American for inventing effective symbols? How does the inventing person recognize the effective use of symbols in a multiethnic society? What are the structuring considerations?

A speaker governs the use of language under tutelage from the audience, for it is the audience that determines effectiveness. Therefore, when King said "I've been to the Mountaintop" to a black audience in Memphis, it was something he would not perhaps—rhetorically speaking—have said if he had been speaking before a white audience at, say, Harvard Law School. The constraints upon him were ethnically or culturally determined. Black audiences demand to hear certain expressions, to see certain things, and to enjoy certain kinds of humor. Proverbs are also a part of the African American speaker's context, and good speakers find in their audiences the commonplaces that are appealing. To say that is to say something about the "folk talk" in the black community, whether it is "Your momma sure was good to me" or "Brothers and Sisters, we got a Rock on our side. Pray with me."

In yet another turn upon the scope of the context, arguments and stylistic devices must be chosen within a certain framework by the black speaker. Despite the seemingly infinite variations upon language, the number of arguments are contextually constrained. Little wonder that the arguments of Martin Luther King and James Farmer in the late 1950s sounded like arguments of William Whipple in the 1830s; or that the positions taken by Malcolm X and Stokely Carmichael (Kwame Toure) were similar to those of Henry Highland Garnet and David Walker over a century before. Listen to Garnet in 1843:

> Two hundred and twenty seven years ago the first of our injured race were brought to the shores of America. They came not with their own consent, to find an unmolested

enjoyment of the blessings of this fruitful soil. The first dealings they had with men calling themselves Christians exhibited to them the worst features of corrupt and sordid hearts: and convinced them that no cruelty is too great, no villainy and no robbery too abhorrent for even enlightened men to perform, when influenced by avarice and lust. Neither did they come flying upon the wings of liberty to a land of freedom. But they came with broken hearts, from their beloved native land, and were doomed to unrequited toil and deep degradation.[28]

This is the speech of a man who knew the horrors of American slavery and whose intense convictions brought forth a flood of protest.

What Garnet knew about America, Malcolm X also knew, and in the following statement Malcolm X put it more succinctly, perhaps more directly:

I'm not going to sit at your table and watch you eat, with nothing on my plate, and call myself a diner. Sitting at the table doesn't make you a diner, unless you eat some of what's on the plate. Being here in America doesn't make you an American. Being born here in America doesn't make you an American.[29]

David Walker had expressed his hatred of the deeds of the "white Christian Americans" in *An Appeal to the Colored Citizens of the World*. In a speech in Boston in 1828, he said:

The dejected, degraded and now enslaved children of Africa will have, in spite of all of their enemies, to take their stand among the nations of the earth.[30]

Walker—like Garnet, Carmichael, and Malcolm X—believed that the rise of Africans in America would be inevitable. Of course, changes in minute detail of style were present, but the external reality with which these black rhetors dealt was basically unchanged. There could be no enlargement of argumentative possibilities for the black speaker without the corresponding enlargement—or better, alteration—of the external reality. Black language and communication are framed by characteristic practices that are products of a special experience, environment, and heritage.

The contemporary cry, "Revolution now, education later!" in the South African townships shows the same response to external realities exhibited in the United States in the 1960s. A host of black speakers in South Africa have used powerfully dramatic language, hoping to shake the firmly established structure of white supremacy. The difficulty is that the appeal from within the metaphoric mind of white culture is tied to many of the assumptions of that culture. In effect, to make an appeal for liberation, political rights, and equality of blacks on the basis of Afrikaner Christian values is to be enslaved to the framework. I contend that change comes from altering circumstances or replacing the frameworks that created the conditions. In South Africa as in the United States, conceptual questions must assume a greater prominence.

The Lyrical Code

The making of a linguistic code is a cultural creation of a people's heritage. How ideas have been structured in the past dictates, to a large extent, how they will be structured in the future. Nuances are transmitted with the general fabric of the mores of a society. The three components to code structuring in the rhetorical behavior of black Americans are lyrical quality, vocal artifact, and indirection.

The African American's approach to language is principally lyrical, and this is the basic poetic and narrative response to reality. Numerous examples have been descriptively documented indicating the expressive quality of the preacher as the prototype of the black speaker. But it is not only the preacher who combines brilliant imagination with music to make it a lyrical style; this combination also predominates among public platform orators whose roots are firmly in the secular rhetoric of the urban streets. The closer a person moves to the white community psychologically, the further he moves from the lyrical approach to language. Among organizing patterns for platform speaking, narration is the most consistent form for a lyrical attitude. Thus the narrative, as similar as it appears to be to the African storyteller's constructions, is nevertheless most consonant with a lyrical approach to language. For example, consider James Weldon Johnson's famous rendition of an African American sermon:

THE CREATION

And God stepped out on space,
And he looked around and said:
I'm lonely—
I'll make me a world.

And far as the eye of God could see
Darkness covered everything,
Blacker than a hundred midnights
Down in a cypress swamp.

Then God smiled,
And the light broke,
And the darkness rolled up on one side,
And the light stood shining on the other,
And God said: That's good!

Then God reached out and took the light in his hands,
And God rolled the light around in his hands
Until he made the sun;
And he set that sun a-blazing in the heavens.
And the light that was left from making the sun
God gathered it up in a shining ball
And flung it against the darkness,
Spangling the night with the moon and stars.
Then down between
The darkness and the light

He hurled the world;
And God said: That's good!

Then God himself stepped down—
And the sun was on his right hand,
And the moon was on his left;
The stars were clustered about his head,
And the earth was under his feet.
And God walked, and where he trod
His footsteps hollowed the valleys out
And bulged the mountains up.

Then he stopped and looked and saw
That the earth was hot and barren.
So God stepped over to the edge of the world
And he spat out the seven seas—
He batted his eyes, and the lightnings flashed—
He clapped his hands, and the thunders rolled—
And the waters above the earth came down,
The cooling waters came down.

Then the green grass sprouted,
And the little red flowers blossomed,
The pine tree pointed his finger to the sky,
And the oak spread out his arms,
The lakes cuddled down in the hollows of the ground,
And the rivers ran down to the sea;
And God smiled again,
And the rainbow appeared,
And curled itself around his shoulder.

Then God raised his arm and he waved his hand
Over the sea and over the land,
And he said: Bring forth! Bring forth!
And quicker than God could drop his hand,
Fishes and fowls
And beasts and birds
Swam the rivers and the seas,
Roamed the forests and the woods,

And split the air with their wings.
And God said: That's good!

Then God walked around,
And God looked around
On all that he had made.
He looked at his sun,
And he looked at his moon,
And he looked at his little stars;
He looked on his world
With all its living things,
And God said: I'm lonely still.

Then God sat down—
On the side of a hill where he could think;
By a deep, wide river he sat down;
With his head in his hands,
God thought and thought,
Till he thought: I'll make me a man!

Up from the bed of the river
God scooped the clay;
And by the bank of the river
He kneeled him down;
And there the great God Almighty
Who lit the sun and fixed it in the sky,
Who flung the stars to the most far corner of the night,
Who rounded the earth in the middle of his hand;
This Great God,
Like a mammy bending over her baby,
Kneeled down in the dust
Toiling over a lump of clay
Till he shaped it in his own image;

Then into it he blew the breath of life,
And man became a living soul.
Amen. Amen.[31]

There is little wonder that our preachers are famous for sermons with titles such as "Dry Bones in the Valley," "The Three Hebrew Boys," "Daniel in the Lion's Den," "The Prodigal Son." These lyrically pregnant stories are demonstratively presented with emphatic diversions to instruct audiences. They are not unlike the narratives of Ananse or Brer Rabbit in their transmission of values and ideas. In fact, it may be argued, in a Herskovitian fashion, that these folk preachers retained for the African audiences the basic elements of the storytellers and, by applying their skills to new materials, made the proverbs and folktales operative in an alien context. The Afro-American speaker exhibits strong tendencies towards a lyrical approach to language, which is structured accordingly.

The power of the lyricism that dances in the sermons of the black preacher derives its vitality from two sources, and Hamilton correctly identifies one source as the oral tradition:

> The black culture is characterized by an oral tradition. Knowledge, attitudes, ideas, notions are traditionally transmitted orally, not through the written word. It is not unusual, then, that the natural leader among black people would be one with exceptional oratorical skills. He must be able to talk, to speak—to preach. In the black religious tradition, the successful black preacher is an expert orator. His role involves more, however. His relationship with his parishioners is reciprocal; he talks to them, and they talk back to him. That is expected. In many church circles this talk-back during a sermon is a firm measure of the preacher's effectiveness.[32]

An aspect of the oral tradition is the polyrhythms of the speech situation. The talk-back, hand clapping, and affirmations represent the complex movement of a whole audience towards unity with the speaker's message. Sometimes the audience shouts "That's right!" "Preach the truth!" "Yes, Lord!" "Help him, my Lord!" "Lordy, Lordy, Lord!" and "Make it plain!" Interspersing the speech with such interjections, the audience gives the speaker immediate feedback to complete the call-and-response patterns of the culture.

The lyricism, according to Henry Mitchell, "is traceable to Black African culture."[33] Moreover, Africa is at the heart of *all* African American behavior. Communication styles are reflective of the internal mythic clock, the epic memory, the psychic stain of Africa in our spirits. This is no great mystery inasmuch as similar memories exist in other people who maintain, however tangentially, a connection with their ancestral traditions. While African Americans may not consciously identify the lyricism with Africa, it is nevertheless a significant part of the communicative pattern, adding the elements of indirection and polyrhythms. In effect, the oral tradition and the call-and-response are both related to the African origin of the cultural behaviors. In this sense, they may be parts of the same phenomenon.

Another aspect of code structuring has to do with how the speaker uses voice—the idea that words and their sounds are products of human work and are, by this virtue, artifactitious. One understands that voice, much like the calimba, fontonfrom, or flute, is merely an instrument for the conveying of ideas. There is no music, only tools for expressing concepts. When one speaks of the orator, as I do, it is necessary to see that, in the African culture, voice is an instrument just as significant as the lexical items spoken. Some lexical items cannot be powerful until they are powerfully spoken by the orator.

I believe that the difference between the European and the African understanding on this subject is profound. To "play jazz," you must have something to say or else you merely play music. The technical procession through the notes is not music as understood in African culture; the use of a technical style, dry and unimaginative, is not oratory. One must know how to use the voice. Intonation and tonal styling are substantive parts of most African American oratory. And the intelligent speaker knows that speaking is an emotional as well as an intellectual process, and that how one alters a phoneme or a word in vocal expression is significant. To know how to say "cat" or "man" is to know the secrets of word magic.

In such a sense, the black speaker knows what the ancestors knew with their use of *nommo:* that all magic is word magic, and the generation and transformation of sounds contribute to a speaker's power. Thus, we are ready to say that whatever a speaker does with a word is a fact unto itself, apart from any reality the word has separate from the particular speaker. A speaker can alter the meaning of a word—"basically the [same] way one can change the word *yeh* from simple response to stern challenge simply by moving the tongue slightly."[34] There are a number of one-syllable sounds that enhance or complement the African American speaker's timbre and pitch: "cat," "say," "man," "yeh," "hey," "what," "right," etc. What is unusual about these sounds is the specificity that accompanies them. Like the black preacher, the disc jockey who lives in the spirit of the people knows precisely what and how to say something.

The contemporary black disc jockey, like the rap musicians and the deejay rockers of Jamaica, operate out of the same collective Afrocentric response to words. In the United States, the rap was preceded by *signifying*. The "signifying monkey," which is legendary in the African American communication memory, gives birth to several forms of signifying, to rapping, and to variations of the "dozens." A common version of the signifying monkey goes like this:

> Down in the jungle near a dried-up creek
> The signifying monkey hadn't slept for a week
> Remembering the ass-kicking he had got in the past
> He had to find somebody to kick the lion's ass.
> The monkey said to the lion one bright summer day,
> There's a bad motherfucker over the way.
> The way he talks about you can't be right.
> And when y'all meet there's bound to be a fight.
> He talks about your mother in a helluva way.
> He called her a no-good bitch and he meant it for a fight.

Now if you ask me, I'll say, "man, it ain't right."
Off went the lion in a terrible rage
creating a breeze which shook the trees
and knocked the giraffe to his knees.
He confronted the elephant up under the tree,
and said, "motherfucker, it's you or me."
He drove at the elephant and made his pass.
That's when the elephant knocked him flat on his ass.
He kicked and stomped him all in his face
Busted two ribs and pulled his tail out of place.
They cursed and fought damn near all day.
I still don't see how that lion got away.[35]

Spoken with the melodious cadence of the poet, the signifying monkey, which is related to the tale of the lion and the rabbit from West Africa, becomes a ritualized form of aggression. The monkey, whose power is insignificant in relationship to the herds of the forest, knows how to neutralize those who possess greater physical power. In this way the African American, using the spiritual ancestor memory of African rhythms and tales, creates a reality through spoken language.

Paul Carter Harrison says in *The Drama of Nommo* that the signifying monkey "reflects the transformation of oral expression as the word passed from the south and caught up with the rhythms of the urban north."[36] The transformation referred to by Harrison is demonstrated in the cadences, rhythms, and lyricisms of black verbal art. In many instances, there is a profound immediacy in the artistic magic of saying something with meaning that is the same as saying something with feeling.

Jahn has understood the interrelationship between the art and activity in most African cultures, continental and diasporan. His appreciation of the aesthetic differences between Europe and Africa, for example, is revealing and helpful in our discussion of sound in the African American speech. Jahn says "an African aesthetic rests, therefore, on the aesthetics of Kuntu, and that means, on the harmony of meaning and rhythm, of sense and form."[37] He contends that the Europeans see the "work" as an object that *has* meaning and rhythm. But the African sees *kuntu* (art) in action: the poem as recited, the carving in its function as stimulus in the worship of an *orisha*, the mask in movement of the dance—that is, when it is *kuntu*. That is why oratory in African cultures is never a thing but always activity. Sound conveys the artistic attitude of the orator.[38]

Furthermore, sound is a rhetorical artifact inasmuch as it has a certain effect upon the hearers. Thus, when a speaker concludes a speech, the statement "He sure sounds good" is a proper approbation. A listener states approval of the energy (form and context being inseparable) expended in the speech. But the approbation is made with particular understanding of what glides and flights of sound were made. Effectiveness, therefore, is dependent upon vocal expression as a lasting impact, not upon gesture or supporting evidence, for obviously a speaker may claim evidence and perfect gesticulation and not be effective. Conversely, by appropriately modulating tones, a speaker can make the evidence and gesticulation accomplish the ends.

The third component to code structuring, observable in stylistic development, is *indirection*. In speaking before an audience, the African American speaker often approaches the central issues of talk in a circuitous fashion, in the manner of the cultural temperament, with lyricism and indirection. By "stalking" the issues, the speaker demonstrates skill and arouses hearers' interest. The person who goes directly to the issues is said to have little imagination and even less flair for rhetorical style.

Indirection is usually a matter of deduction, as the speaker toys with related ideas and concepts before focusing on his prime target:

> I am not a Politician, nor the son of a Politician
> I am not a Republican, nor a Democrat
> Nor an American.[39]

In this typical passage from Malcolm X we see the formula for indirection. What could have been simply put as "I know that I am not an American" is more elaborately clothed. Such embellishment in public speaking can also be derived from the speaker's metaphorical capabilities, or illustrations, or aphorisms, or a combination of these techniques. But whatever the speaker's choice, he is certainly playing in the right ball park if he "surrounds" his issue before focusing upon it. This behavior is true not only of the platform speaker, but also plays a role in dyadic conversation. Its true bases are the enthymematic products of our cultural experiences. One would be mistaken to speak of this linguistic behavior as "beating around the bush," because it is always *on* the bush, though at times tapping it exceedingly lightly.

Herskovits was one of the first to observe the use of indirection in black language. He comments in *The Myth of the Negro Past* that indirection may have been a characteristic the African Americans brought with them from Africa. In one example of the African fondness for indirection, the attitude of the French colonial authorities in Africa was shown to be unwise because of their straightforward manner. When the French directly asked, for tax purposes, how many people lived in the houses of each compound, the old people would respond that they were wiser than to ask a person directly to tell something that is a disadvantage to himself. Herskovits says:

> Whatever the African basis for this attitude, it must be made clear that slavery did nothing to diminish the force of its sanctions. Nor have the disabilities under which the negro has lived since slavery tended to decrease its appeal as an effective measure of protection. Nonetheless, certain characteristic reactions to life in Africa itself—on the part of the upper class as well as ordinary folk, which even take certain institutionalized forms in the political system of at least one well integrated African culture—make it essential that this tradition of indirection be regarded as a carry-over of aboriginal culture.[40]

Herskovits is convinced that African Americans came to America "equipped with the technique" of indirection.[41] Any Afrocentric analysis of black communication must consider the importance of limited revelation, holding back on what one knows, restraint in speaking directly to strangers in the African American culture. Of course, in contemporary society one has to consider also the influence of acculturation on black style.

The Art of Improvisation

Discourse spoken by African Americans is characterized by artistic instrumentation. As an art form, the speech, frequently interrupted by vocal responses from the hearers, is *made* with careful attention to effect. Like African art of the highest order, it is functional and is not made for art's sake alone but for its practical value to people.[42] Therefore, when audiences respond with outbursts of "Amen," "That's right," "Tell the Truth," etc., they are testifying to the impact of the delivery of the message. It is difficult to refer to these vocal outbursts as interruptions of the speech; more accurately, they are affirmations.

Speakers who succeed in arousing in their audiences the desire to give vocal assent are prototypes for the black community. And the audiences' vocal affirmations, which are regulatory, comprise a monitoring system (as feedback systems generally do) for effectiveness. This is similar to the common function of applause during certain American cultural events. When a speaker views delivery of a message as a performance, certain constraints and possibilities, which otherwise would *not* be, are placed upon him. Here, then, it is not just the linguistic code that a speaker must be concerned with, but presence as a speaker (appearance, countenance, grace, and manner). And presence is integrally related to how a person chooses to argue, contend, affirm, or entertain; and how the listener chooses to respond to his language. By using language common to the audiences, a speaker is not merely understandable, he is credible. This explains the success of folk preachers and some radical orators. But delivery, however animated, cannot substitute for a speaker's genuine sensitivity to audiences. This holds for every dyadic communication situation, whether speaker to audiences (many) or speaker to listener (one).

The kind of delivery indicates how a speaker regards the situation and audiences; that is, the choice of physical styles— *pompous* or *conversational*—reflects the rhetorical setting. Furthermore, the choice of modes—*impromptu, manuscript, extemporaneous,* or *memorized*—underscores the effect of situation and audiences upon the speaker. The typical rhetorical setting is persuasive and the proper decisions of the speaker influence the persuasive impact on audiences. As a consideration for a metatheory of African American black language and communication, it should be noted that our speakers generally prefer the extemporaneous mode of delivery, characterized by lively speaking and the coining of exact language at the moment of utterance. In oratory, as in music, the individualistic, the improvisational, is the soul of performance. This is not to say that memorized speeches are unheard of, or that manuscript speeches are not given. When exactness of language and careful timing are essential, the speaker must react in the most appropriate manner. In most cases, the manuscript speech serves a speaker's needs of exactness and definite timing. While presentation of a message is constrained by environmental conditions, it completes the speech act for the encoding person and is therefore essential to communication.

Just as with jazz, which is the classical music of America, the improvised voice, with spontaneity and variety, is the voice of African American oratory. An endless variety of presentation styles, all falling within the acceptable Afrocentric motif, speaks to the diversity of the orators, from Booker T. Washington to Louis Farrakhan. Their province is the spoken word, and in this province they excel at presentation of the message. This should not be confused with white styles, whose sources are different; the Afrocentric presentation forms are related to music, particularly the epic styles of blues and jazz.

The forms may be seen further back, in the work songs, which predate the blues, spirituals, and jazz. In these folk-forms one finds the call-and-response, improvisation, and rhythm.

The political and cultural symbols of American society reflect the monoethnicity that has persisted in American cultural phenomena. Spoken discourse as conceptualized and as practiced apart from the new directions outlined above (frame of mind, context, structure of code, and delivery) is demonstratively unrepresentative symbolically. What is needed is an expansion of cultural perspectives and a reconceptualization of symbolic engineering in order to understand the role of African culture in African American behavior. Inasmuch as our perception of people, events, and objects can influence language, we surely must be cognizant that beyond the level of specific words in language that are monoethnic there are substantive influences upon language (a sort of Whorfian twist) that make our communicative habits sterile. The writers who have argued that the English language is our enemy have argued convincingly on the basis of "*black*ball," "*black*mail," "*black* Friday," etc.; but they have not argued thoroughly in terms of the total symbolic architecton of society. Only when we challenge the symbolic generation of monoethnic concepts in a multicultural society will we truly make progress.

As Eleanor W. Traylor shows in her essay on Toni Morrison's *Tar Baby*, Europeans have often imposed their symbols on blacks.

> The people of this fable-world imbibe toxic ideas . . . they are miseducated by cant; by historical, cultural, and political bias or ignorance of schoolish books; by insidious daily-diet propaganda sponsored by moneymongers; . . . by foolish slogans rampant in this world convincing many that "if you White, you right; if you Black, stand back or catchup."[43]

The imposition of a single symbol system onto a multiethnic society typifies the Eurocentrism in the conventional approach to language. By accepting the constituents of the African American communication patterns, we extend the understanding of human communication. On the other hand, it is difficult to have meaningful discourse when the points of reference are inherently biased. In fact, symbol imperialism, rather than institutional racism, is the major social problem facing multicultural societies. It is both linguistic and rhetorical in our use of communication. Santa Claus as an American symbol is one example. In terms of discourse, our perceptions of Santa Claus color our responses. As an ethnic symbol imposed as a universal symbol of benevolence, Santa is not adequate. But neither is Hanu-Claus, nor is Saint Soul—two versions of the symbol developed by ethnic and racial minority groups. Only a reevaluation of the constituents of communication for a multiethnic society can establish meaningful dialogue. "Flesh"-color Band-Aids, traditional American combs, sunglasses or regular eyeglasses, or the nude look—all of which disregard racial variations in skin color and bone structure—are indicative of such symbol imperialism. Language is the instrument of conveyance of attitudes and perceptions, and these symbols must play havoc with symbolic structure.

One can illustrate this point almost endlessly, but that is not my objective here. However, it should be sufficient to say that most of the so-called universal concepts fail transculturally, and without transcultural validity there is not universality. This is precisely the point Armstrong makes against Jung's archetypes.[44] Jung's archetypes could not be called universal because they could not be seen as classes of events across cultures, regardless of their substantive validity within cultures. Armstrong shows us that both Jung's archetypes and Lévi-Strauss's bipolar archetypes are to be rejected as universal.[45] He concludes that while Jung's archetypes as descriptive categories of the psyches of the Western European may be valid, they cannot be viewed as other than Western and "therefore not per se basic structures of man's mind."[46] This is not to say that archetypes are not possible in African or Asian culture, but only to declare that, unless one can establish transcultural validity for the archetype, it remains substantively culturally defined. Perhaps we should look at how Eurocentric perspectives assisted in the misunderstanding of black language behavior. The imposition of a view that is antithetical to the nature of the language emerged in the 1960s, as a result of a universalist conception.

In the discussion of African American language, some writers have obfuscated the tone and style of Ebonics. Good-natured endeavors to explain the persistence of Ebonics in African American culture have become crippled. In attempting to refute the negative views of black language, some neo-radical linguists of the 1960s adopted the idea of black language as nonstandard and inflicted a confusion about our culture that has proved difficult to eliminate. They not only accepted the dialectical structure of American racist ideology, which sees white as standard and others as nonstandard, even substandard, but borrowed from the twisted formulations of a supremacist logic. Such is the complexity of the material artifact of Ebonics. Hence, B. L. Bailey argued in the 1960s that black people used a nonstandard English.[47] This was not an unusual perspective because in the same journal, R. G. Kaplan, in "On a Note of Protest (in a Minor Key): Bidialectism vs. Bidialectism," expounded a similar position on black language. Kaplan adds a turn to the position, however, by insisting that "non-standard" language was not a racial but an economic issue.[48] Despite Kaplan's intentions, his argument seeks to demonstrate that the preservation of the white power structure is dependent upon the teaching of English grammar as a vehicle for assimilation and standardization; he errs when he does not see the cultural antecedents to Ebonics. The genius of the Africans who created this unique linguistic response to their environment cannot be gainsaid. Yoruba, Asante, Ibo, Hausa, Mandingo, Serere, and Wolof had to combine elements of their language in order to communicate with each other and the English. Ebonics was a creative enterprise, out of the materials of interrelationships and the energies of the African ancestral past.

Those interested in the social and political uses of speech must be flexible enough to accommodate this view. Of course, much has been done in this regard, particularly as it relates to the classroom teacher's understanding of Ebonics and its various dialects. Clearly, the statement of a metatheoretical position for African communication suggests how we can structure our symbols to be more useful. Ethno-rhetorics concerned with exploring the persuasive potentials of languages within certain ethnic/cultural groups may be stimulants for a broader philosophical consideration of symbolic utility for a more humanistic society. Therefore, the fundamental position we must assume is that of making an aggressive beginning, despite the political and economic constraints that tend to ensnare us. Eurocentric systems have functioned as directors of the social systems, holding an enormous grip on the advancement of social and intellectual thought.

I believe that the early black protest speakers understood that there had to be a fundamental refocusing of the social and intellectual environment in order to achieve true liberation. Although the literature of American origin was rich in the language of liberty and freedom, it was always a freedom totally within the framework of the Eurocentric view. This worked for whites from Europe; they could analyze the various possibilities inasmuch as a common cultural thread was shared. However, for the African American this thread represented a whole fabric based upon a strong apocalyptic-Viking mythology. Its exclusivity created (*inter alia*) the need for justifying rhetorics to support it.

Historically, our social and political protests have been emblems of resistance. The struggle has been to show that difference does not have to be oppositional. Quite frankly, this is difficult when the bombarding Eurocentricisms in the social sciences and humanities suggest the inability of the majority of whites to think beyond Eurocentric ideals. A music school that does not teach a course on Duke Ellington, a history department without any mention of Du Bois, or a philosophy department that refuses to consider Fanon or King reflect, in a direct manner, the imbedded abstraction of exclusivity.

African Foundations of *Nommo*

Any interpretation of African culture must begin at once to dispense with the notion that, in all things, Europe is teacher and Africa is pupil. This is the central point of my argument. To raise the question of an imperialism of the intellectual tradition is to ask a most meaningful question as we pursue African rhetoric, because Western theorists have too often tended to generalize from a Eurocentric base. What I seek to demonstrate in this section is the existence of an African concept of communication rooted in traditional African philosophies. Later, I will expand this by referring to a close description and examination of Akan culture, particularly as that culture exemplifies the use of words in the organization of society.

African Public Discourse

Public speaking as practice predates the development of theory, whether in Africa, Asia, or Europe. Both speaking and writing are forms of human interaction. What purpose is served by these forms of communication? The answer to this question speaks of the complex problem of cultural evaluation. For example, writing is used for communication and historical preservation. In some traditional African societies those two ends have been admirably satisfied by the drum. Communication was swift and the range was great; in the event that the first drummer was unable to reach all the persons he wanted to reach, another drummer, at the outer fringes, could take up the message for further transmission. Thus the drummer, along with the village sage, became a repository of all the necessary historical data relating to the village.

In some African societies, such as ancient Meroe, Kemet, and Abyssinia, written documents are extensive. However, in the whole of Africa and the African world, both past and present, there is a vocal-expressive modality that dominates all communication culture. This modality is part of the continuity with the ancient African past. What is of importance to us is that Africans in America maintained an expressive sense that manifested itself as life force in dance, music, and speech. Expression, therefore, is not the captive of the written word; it is the word revealed in life. I use the term *orature* to refer to this phenomenon as the sum total of oral tradition, which includes vocality, drumming, storytelling, praise singing, and naming.

There is, of course, a considerable legacy of writing in Africa. Dating from the earliest book still extant, the *Book of the Going Forth by Night* (called variously the *Egyptian Book of the Dead* and the *Book of the Dead*), writing has been prominent in Africa among priests and royalty. The *adinkra* ideograms of the Asante, the *nsibidi* of the Ejagham, and the sacred symbols of the Benin Obas are but a few examples of African writing. None of the early African writing systems owe anything to Western systems. Even the Bamun system of writing, developed by King Njoya to record the history of his people, is essentially an African creation, despite the fact that the Bamun had contact with foreigners. *Nsibidi* is an Efik writing system that shows no outside or Western influence. Robert Farris Thompson says:

> [T]he moral and civilising impact of *nsibidi* betrays the ethnocentrism of an ideology that would exclude ideographic forms from consideration in the history of literacy. Educated Western persons continue to assume that . . . traditional Africa was culturally impoverished because it lacked letters to record its central myths, ideals, and aspirations. Yet the Ejagham and Ejagham-influenced blacks who elaborated a creole offshoot of *nsibidi* in Cuba have proven otherwise.[49]

Although *nsibidi* is not influenced by Western script, it bears a close resemblance to other African scripts, particularly to ancient *medu netr* (Egyptian). Following Theophile Obenga, I have selected several pictograms that show similarity between the scripts:

Egyptian		Nsibidi	
♀	Running man Messenger	♀	Running man Messenger
⌒	Loaf of bread	⌒	Calabash for food storage
⦵	Serpent		
		ⵔⵔⵔⵔ	Serpent
⌂	Lizard		
		⊿₀	Lizard

B. Niangoran-Bouah has demonstrated, in *The Akan World of Gold Weights: Abstract Design Weights,* that at least seven African languages show an affinity to ancient Egyptian. Published by Les Nouvelles Editions Africaines of Abidjan in 1984, Niangoran-Bouah's work has already become a much-quoted classic. He is fascinated by the similarities of West African scripts to the ancient Egyptian, and believes *nsibidi* to be a key script in understanding the dispersion of the so-called "secret" script to other people. *Nsibidi* has often been called the language of the secret Nsibidi Society; but there are no secret societies in Africa, there are only societies of secrets. The Nsibidi Society used the *nsibidi* writing system to impart nobility, grandeur, erudition, wisdom, and poetry. In Cuba, *nsibidi* was called *anaforuana;* and Thompson says that "these signs are written and rewritten with mantriac power and pulsation. Mediatory forces, the sacred signs of the *anaforuana* corpus, indicate a realm beyond ordinary discourse."[50] Other societies, among different people, possessed their secrets for manhood or womanhood, agriculture, circumcision, astronomy, geometry, healing, and ethics in various ideographic systems.

But it is in the complexity and rhythm of the spoken word that a conception of rhetoric and discourse is most prevalent. An Afrocentric perspective demands examination of the artifacts of African culture from the vantage point of the traditions of Africa. Therefore, it is unproductive to try to explain the concept of the *okyeame* (linguist) from a Eurocentric perspective, particularly when that concept is not present in European culture. Of course, such explanations are often attempted by those who don't understand—like the explanations of white missionaries who, once given hospitality by Africans, wrote in their diaries that the "natives" thought white men were gods. Their conceptions of themselves and their hosts contributed to an inadequate interpretation of hospitality and generosity to strangers.

As we have said, conventional rhetorical theory is not universal; in practice and evaluation, traditional rhetoric is bound to Western society. For example, Cicero's *De Inventione* and Aristotle's *Rhetoric* create a special Western perspective on discourse that in and of itself is no problem. The problem arises when those products are seen as standards for the rest of the world. The works of Ahmed Baba and scholars at the University of Sankore show the importance of discourse in West African society. Yet these works are little known and have hardly any impact on the understanding of rhetoric we have come to accept in the West. Humans who interact vocally with others for the purpose of achieving cooperation have certainly existed in Africa much longer than in Europe or Asia.

Yet interaction in African society proceeds from different bases than interaction in European society. The reason is simple. People respond to the ideal that is concealed in every facet of their existence, and this ideal is determined for them according to different views of life. No one can divest himself or herself of the myths that constitute linkages to a particular historical experience. Michael Bradley, who takes a determinist view of behavior in his book *The Iceman Inheritance*, contends that European attitudes and responses were shaped by the Würm Ice Age.[51] In the European landscape, dominated by glaciers, a mentality (which can easily be called a *caveman* mentality) emerged to draw boundaries, establish patriarchy, and introduce individual and clan territoriality. In the regions where the sun dominated the environment, the "palm tree mentality" (to use Leonard Jeffries' expression) emerged. This world view is fundamentally community/society-oriented, relaxed, and directed towards transcendence. Pressures of human survival, xenophobia, and reliance on hunting combined to create the philosophical outlook of the European. On the other hand, interaction between humans in African society, based on agriculture, burial of the dead, and ancestor respect, relates to another tradition. One could therefore discuss the African view of communication as an example of a human behavior affected by a strong collective mentality, where the group was more important than the individual.

Rhetoric as Functional Art

First, let us establish the dimensions of public speaking in any society. To stimulate one's fellow to cooperative action through the use of language is no mean task; it requires skill, knowledge of human nature, and the necessary physical organs to utter sounds. Skill implies a certain technical proficiency, an ability to use one's knowledge effectively. Thus the interrelationship of skill and knowledge of human nature is clearly the basis of any meaningful venture in public speaking. I argue, then, that public discourse is an art. But art is produced by a systematic application of skill in effecting a given result; of course, we could extend that to include the craft, occupation, or activity requiring such skill. Suffice it to say: While it has been made plain by rhetoricians, and I tend to agree, that rhetoric is concerned with the systematic observation and classification of facts and the establishment of verifiable general principles, not even the most Eurocentric writer can dispense with the conceptions of public discourse as art.

African art is never *l'art pour l'art;* it is always functional. The reason it is functional is that the work is "constituted, in a primordial and intransigent fashion, of basic cultural psychic conditions—not symbols of those conditions but specific enactments—presentations—of those very conditions."[52] This is true whether we are speaking of music, sculpture, or oratory.

There can be no art without a functional objective within the mind of the artist, whose work must do something, perform something, or say something. Public discourse as an art form can only be complete when it is productive and, hence, functional. The difference between this position and the position of the European view of art seems profound. While it is common for neo-Aristotelian rhetoricians to emphasize the observers in the judgment of discourse, Africans highlight the creative process of the artist. To be an observer is to be primarily interested in the product, but to be an artist means that the creation and its function in society are uppermost. Thus the African sees the discourse as the creative manifestation of what is *called to be*. That which is *called to be*, because of the mores and values of the society, becomes the created thing; and the artist, or speaker, satisfies the demands of the society by calling into being that which is functional. Functionality, in this case, refers to the object (sculpture, music, poem, dance, speech) that possesses a meaning within the communicator's and audience's world view; a meaning that is constructed from the social, political, and religious moments in the society's history.

In such a view of art, public discourse becomes a power, and the fundament of rhetoric is not the discourse-object but the creative attitude of the speaker. To say that public discourse becomes a power is only to emphasize the activity aspect of the discourse in African thought. One cannot speak of a speech as an object but of speech as an attitude. The power of effective action is the force of the public discourse; and the speaker who makes a speech never completes a discourse as object because completeness is to be found in action. That specific continental African societies understood this, I shall demonstrate subsequently in a discussion of Akan customs.

Now that we have said African art is never for its own sake, it is possible to say a few words about the relationship between society and the public discourse. What is the meaning of the speech in traditional African society? In what sense can the speech be said to fit into the ethnic cosmogony? These are not easy questions to answer, and yet it seems that the answers lie somewhere in the realms of African personality theory or African culture. Several scholars have recently attempted exploration of conceptual systems, theories of personality and culture related to Africa. It is as easy to speak of an "African mind" as it is to speak of an "Oriental temperament," and for some of the same reasons. When we speak of Africans, we are usually talking about a multitude of attitudes, peoples, and cosmologies; and in this circumstance, to speak of an African mind is to speak cautiously. Nevertheless, we speak broadly of traditional African society—perhaps, even African culture.

African society is essentially a society of harmonies, inasmuch as the coherence or compatibility of persons, things, and modalities is at the root of traditional African philosophy. Several scholars have commented on the nature of traditional African law as concerned with the restoration of equilibrium.[53] In customary African law, establishment of guilt is not the primary consideration of law but, rather, the restoration of communal balance and, therefore, peace.[54] In fact, Adesanya, a Nigerian writer, declares that "this is not simply a coherence of fact or faith, nor of reason and traditional beliefs, nor of reason and contingent facts, but a coherence or compatibility among all disciplines."[55] The concatenation of everything is so tight that to subtract one item is to paralyze the system.

Wole Soyinka's autobiography, *Ake: The Years of Childhood*,[56] is an intricate view of Nigerian society in confrontation, yet there is the eternal quest for harmony in Soyinka's other works. It is remarkable for us to understand that, given Soyinka's intellectual accommodation in two societies, one essentially African and the other European, it is possible for him to transcend, by the grace of Ogun, this duality and establish in *Ake*, as he does in *Death and the King's Horseman*, the African desire, despite the Western interference, for harmony. In *Ake* there are smells, sensations, rhythms, mystery— all moving in unison with fiery spark-headed spirits, a drunken uncle, an articulate father and a wild Christian mother. Soyinka combines the Yoruba traditional with the Western traditional, saving—perhaps—the world, *his* world, from collapse. His is a coherent and arresting portrait, despite the struggles of Obatala and Ogun with Jesus and Peter.

The public discourse, therefore, cannot exist apart from the mutual compatibility of the traditional world view. In force, active form and content operating harmoniously, the speech is logically linked to the society as in Soyinka's experiences. Obviously, this type of society appears rigid and constricting to many Western peoples, but, on the other hand, in customary African society the human possibilities are abundant. The difference lies in two varied conceptions of the speech and the speaker. Merriam has written that "in Euro-American Society there is a tendency to compartmentalize the arts and to divorce them from aspects of everyday life; thus we have 'pure' art as opposed to 'applied' art as well as the 'artist' and 'commercial artist' or 'craftsmen,' who are also differentiated both in role and in function."[57] However, for the Afrocentricist, the speech is a functioning and integral part of the society and cannot be separated from the entire world view because the word-power is indeed the generative power of the community.[58]

Additionally, traditional African philosophy cannot make the distinction of "speaker" and "audience" to the same degree found in rhetorical traditions of Euro-American society. Separateness of speaker or artist from audience in Euro-American society is based upon the degree of participation. But in African society the coherence among persons and things accords, so that music, dance, or *nommo* must be a collective activity. Melville Herskovits' observation that distinctions of artist and audience are foreign to traditional African culture ("Art is a part of life, not separated from it")[59] does not mean that there are no individual speakers or artists, but rather that their performance becomes a collective experience. In neo-African culture as expressed in North and South America, one gets the feel of this group performance in religious meetings and, indeed, in some secular gatherings. What are conventionally labelled reactions and responses of the audience might be better understood if we spoke of these phenomena as collective actions of participants. Afro-Americans, viewing a movie, are participating in the events of that movie, not in the oral interpretation sense of "fulfilling the potential" but in creating the potential. The potential does not exist apart from the participants; thus when an actor or actress is "being seen" on the movie screen, the "audience" is being seen.

African rhetoric is distinguished not only in its concern for coherence and participation but also in its relationship to the stability of the traditional society. Mutual compatibility of the several aspects of a philosophical perspective is only one benefit of coherence; another is the efficient and nonconfrontational operation of the village. In instances of conflict or disagreement among members of the society, public discourse must function to restore the stability that conflict creates. I shall mention later how this is handled among the Akan, but let me say for now that within the speech, the speaker is constantly restoring the internal harmony of the discourse through tone, volume, and rhythm. Delivery becomes, for the traditional African speaker, an opportunity to engage in a textual as well as a contextual search for harmony. The stability of the community is essential, and public speaking, when used in connection with conflict solution, must be directed towards maintaining community harmony. As a microcosmic example of the traditional African society's base in the harmony of all parts, the meaningful public discourse manifests rhetorical agreeableness in all its parts, ceremonial and actual.

The libator, for example, in the culture of the Ga people of West Africa, is typical of the attempt of the orator to seek harmony. In effect, the libator's place is much like the role of the orator in Western culture, yet the libator is much more a member of a collective consciousness. According to Abarry, the libator is a poet, a creative genius capable of assuming trance-like dispositions.[60] Only the libator in African culture, rich in the history of traditions of his people, assumes a completely poetic nature. In the performance of libation, the libator exploits oratorical and poetical techniques to reinforce his message or to enhance his natural gifts. As in many African societies, the libation is an intricate part of Ga society. The people are united by it with the ancestors; by it, the community is shown its relationship to posterity.

In the process of ritualizing an event, the libator normally holds a special vessel with the liquid of libation, usually liquor, in both hands as he approaches the audience. This is a solemn, reverent act, demonstrating sincerity before the deities whom the libator seeks to honor. The libator may be flanked by elders, a sort of choral amen corner, as he begins his libation. They shout, "May it be so" as he speaks. This response is similar to the African American interjections of "Yes, Lord," "Speak the Truth," "Say it, Rev," and "Make it plain," often heard in the African American church.

An assistant would normally fill the libatory vessel, as needed, from a bottle he carries with him. Bells, horns, or drums are frequently played on these occasions, as "surrogates," to sustain the rhythm of the libator's verse. A harmonious interplay between the surrogates and the libator suggests the call-and-response pattern of Africans in the Americas. There is no subservience of content to form here. Musical instruments are the extensions of the body—the hands, the voice—forever emphasizing the ascendancy of natural talent over technical skill, spontaneity over rules, and accidents over rigid form. Expression, which recognizes that externals are more like effects while internals are like causes, is maximized. Such a view of the libatory function is synthetic, not analytic: the bringing together of ancestral spirits, the supreme God, and living people in one place. The libator achieves this purpose through invocation, supplication, and conclusion. As he invokes the ancestors, the gods, and the Supreme Deity, he pours some of the liquor on the ground.

Libation, one of the purest forms of the African word magic,

combines all elements of structure, style, invention, generation, and the productive capacity of sound that are found in
the best African oratory.

Expressive Sound

Sound is evocative and its mystical powers evoke psychic
forces. In the Yoruba legend of Odu-ifa, Ogundosee became
Irunmole, the one who possesses musical genius. Ogundosee
is therefore the one who imparts musical ability and style.
Furthermore, the Yoruba Odu-ifa, Owonrin Meji, has a verse
that goes:

> Orun me gbà á á
> Orun mi gbò ó ó
>
> My essence emanates from loud sound
> My essence emanates from thunderous sound

This Yoruba insistence on sound as essence must not be confused with Walter Ong's concept of sound. Ong describes the
world of oral/aural categories as dynamic because sound always tells us that something is happening, that some force is
operating.[61] Ong believes that "illiterate man" recognizes
something is coming and going in sound, a recognition that
the literate do not possess.[62]

By the nature of traditional African philosophy, rhetoric in
African society is an architectonic functioning art, continu-
ously fashioning the sounds and symbols of the people even as
it reenacts history. The *word* is productive and imperative,
calling forth and commanding. Its power derives from the
traditional emphasis of fashioning harmony out of spoken
materials. Words, as spoken by the chief or physician, may be
effective because of the station, assigned or inherited, of the
speaker, even though power inheres in vocal communication.
The centrality of the word has existed for a long time in Af-

rican communities. As Jahn explains, "[T]he central significance of the word in African culture is not a phenomenon of
one particular time."[63] Furthermore,

> If there were no word, all forces would be frozen, there
> would be no procreation, no change, no life. "There is
> nothing that there is not; whatever we have a name for,
> that is," so speaks the wisdom of the Yoruba priests. The
> proverb signifies that the naming, the enunciation pro-
> duces what it names. Naming is an incantation, a crea-
> tive act. What we cannot conceive of is unreal; it does not
> exist. But every human thought, once expressed, becomes
> reality. For the word holds the course of things in train
> and changes and transforms them. And since the word
> has this power, every word is an effective word, every
> word is binding.[64]

Thus, because the word is imperative, it is the fundament
as well as the fashioning instrument of traditional African society. All religion, music, medicine, and dance are produced
by vocal expression, inasmuch as creativity is called into existence by man speaking. There is also a correlation between
the effectiveness of the word and the power of the speaker as
expressed by his personality and status. The more powerful
the priest, the stronger his incantations and invocations. But
no priest can exist apart from the word; indeed, without the
word, nothing can be, for the word creates reality.

The overwhelming importance of expression in African culture puts a heavy burden on the ability to hear and see. Intricacies in verbal expressions are evidence of genius. Expression possesses this place of significance in speech as well as in
music in African society, and the interrelationship of the two
expressive genres is well established. All study of African music requires verbal emphasis, as well as demonstration, because of the power of the expressive word.[65] Furthermore, the
commonality of pitch, rate, volume, duration, and message
content makes speech and music parts of the same expressive

pattern. Wachsmann contends that "in Africa a useful working hypothesis is that there is little music that does not have some affinity with words."[66] Since the "word principle" is behind all production and generation, it is possible to consider it as an architectonic system that gives existence to all things. Transformation is accomplished when a speaker employs words in any social situation, in an attempt to bring about harmonious relationships within the traditional society. Whether the specific situation is an interpersonal conflict mediated by a chief, *okyeame,* or village elder, a natural disaster, or an attempt to persuade villagers to follow a certain course of action, transformation is sought through the *expressive* word.[67] In this sense, we can speak of an African architecton that influences communal behavior, which, in fact, is the source and origin of that behavior.

The Akan Example

Examination of the Akan principles surrounding communication reveals the extent of the African architecton in a traditional society. The Akan, who live in present-day Ghana, include the Asante, Fanti, Brong-Ahafo, and other groups. In Akan society, the *okra,* the *sunsum,* and the *mogya* constitute the totality of an individual. All communal behavior is influenced by this architecton. In the *okra* we find the guiding principle of a person's destiny, the spirit that remains with a person until death. It is from this conception of human reality that the Akan people form their expressive word.

The Akan believe that it is possible to delineate, from the individual's behavioral system, that which represents the *okra*. In other words, there is an identifiable message system, in the total behavioral system of any Akan, that constitutes the image of the *okra*. The most distinguishing characteristic of the *okra* is its *unpredictability*. The *okra* also represents intuitive knowledge, and such knowledge can be good or bad. Thus, all creative insights are attributed to the *okra*. Similarly, all bizarre behaviors can be characterized as the activation of the *okra*. People whose behaviors are consistently impulsive or bizarre are said to possess "bad" *okra*. Consequently, when a person speaks in a way that the hearer cannot follow or performs an oath contrary to harmony, it is because of a problem with his *okra*.

The *okra* acts as the link between humans and the community of the supernatural, or nonhuman spirits, and their relationship with the environment, time, and space. This is the principal representation of the Akan image of a person as a spiritual being. The *okra* is a continuous flow of spiritual energy, capable of manifesting its presence in all human experience. The Akan believe that before a child attains puberty, the father's *ntoro* or *bosom* acts as the child's *sunsum*—the spiritual substance responsible for genius, temper, and character. It is the educable part of the person because it is adaptive. Thus, the *ntoro* represents reasoning and reasoned intelligence, controlling and controlled feeling, and calculating and calculated or planning and planned action. The *sunsum* of *ntoro*, representing both curiosity and precision, reflects a unique balance between objectivity and subjectivity. Indeed, the Akan consider pure objective human reasoning impossible. This belief is expressed in the saying, "There is always some blood in the head of the tsetse fly." The Akan's conception of the individual is inextricably linked to the image of the group, and the ingenuity of Akan social philosophers is derived from their ability to apply the principle of intermediary (*okyeame*) to human interactions. That is why I have called this view of human society *personalism*, as opposed to materialism or spiritualism.

The Akan word *mogya* means blood. The Akan use the word in the biological sense, and it means the fluid circulating in the heart, arteries, and veins of vertebrates. Yet it also refers to spiritual factors symbolized in the principle of ancestor spirits. For example, we say our *mogya* aids us in interpreting traditions, rules, and protocols of community as left by the ancestors.

According to Michael Appiah, the Akan justify membership in the communication communities of the supernatural, ancestral, and enviro-technical worlds by an appeal to the organizing principles of *kra-din, ntoro,* and *mogya.*[68] Appiah's claim can be illustrated by classifying the concepts of *okra, sunsum,* and *mogya* with cultural communities according to principles identified with seven deities that represent the seven days of the week. The deities are members of the supernatural community, and they control the days of the week. Thus, the days of the week are named after the deities:

The deity of Sunday is	Awusi;
The deity of Monday is	Adwo;
The deity of Tuesday is	Bena;
The deity of Wednesday is	Aku;
The deity of Thursday is	Yaw;
The deity of Friday is	Afi;
The deity of Saturday is	Amen.

Therefore, the names of the days of the week are *Kwasida* (Sunday), *Dwoda* (Monday), *Benada* (Tuesday), *Wukuda* (Wednesday), *Yawda* (Thursday), *Fida* (Friday), and *Mememda* (Saturday). The suffix *da* means day.

The philosophical importance of this nomenclature resides in the expressive word for a person, the name, which is central to the person. If there were no name, all personal forces would be static; there would be no possibility of social intercourse, no growth, no development, and no integration into human society. Naming becomes a creative act, a productive architectonic act in personal development.

The Akan's use of the name is similar to the Yoruba's, the Ewe's, and the African American's. While the African American does not maintain the formalized Akan or Yoruba response to naming, one does find the prevalence of nicknames, which serve as markers of the African presence in the "soundsense" of black America. Almost all young men and women

receive nicknames at an early age and these names are des-
ignatory, referring to one's physical appearance (e.g., Red,
Gooseneck, Peanut Head), character (e.g., Bull, Slick, Rap), or
relation (e.g., Buddy, Bro' Boy, Big Sister, and Cool Baby). Rap
songs and poems, such as the one by H. Rap Brown, almost
always announce one of the names of the speaker:

> Man you must don't know who I am.
> I'm sweet peeter jeeter the womb beater
> The baby maker the cradle shaker
> The deerslayer the bookbinder the woman finder
> Known from the Gold Coast to the rocky shores of Maine
> Rap is my name and love is my game.[69]

Although the Akan's use of naming is more formal and structured, the essential idea is the same in African American nicknames and other nonlegal names.

The Akan express the spiritual identity of the individual by
the first name, that is, *kra-din*. The individual's first name
identifies him or her as a member of the supernatural cultural
community. The person's first name is associated with the god
of the day on which he or she is born. In other words, an *okra*
that takes on human form on a given weekday becomes the
servant or messenger of the god on whose day he, the *okra*,
makes his appearance in human form in the living, enviro-
technical communication community. This community is distinguishable from the enviro-spiritual communication community that is the realm of spirit mediums, deities, and ancestors.

The Akan concept of first name, *kra-din*, therefore, is derived from a cross-classification of the concept of *okra*, with
the concepts referring to members of the supernatural communication community. For example, the Akan first name
Kwabena (i.e., *Kwa* = messenger or servant of Bena, the god
of Tuesday) is derived from the interconnection of *okra* and
Bena. While Akan children receive their first names from the
days on which they are born, their surnames are given them

by their fathers. This is normally done eight days after the birth day. The significance of Akan surnames lies in the fact that they symbolize the beginning of one's membership in the community of the living. The accompanying chart illustrates the relationship between the *okra* and *kra-din* and days of the week.

THE LOGIC OF AKAN NAMES

Deity	Day of Week (Akan)	Day of Week (English)	Male Name	Female Name
Awusi	*Kwasida*	Sunday	Kwasi	Akoma or Esi
Adwo	*Dwoda*	Monday	Kwadwo	Adwoa
Bena	*Benada*	Tuesday	Kwabena or Ebo	Abenaa
Aku	*Wukuda*	Wednesday	Kwaku	Akua
Yaw	*Yawda*	Thursday	Yaw or Kwao	Yaa or Aba
Afi	*Fida*	Friday	Kofi	Afua
Amen	*Memenda*	Saturday	Kwame or Kwamena	Amma (Ama)

If an Akan wrote *Wofre me Kwadwo Asante* (They call me Kwadwo Asante), our understanding of this sentence will depend on our understanding of the principles underlying Akan surnames. The surname Asante identifies the person as a member of the community of the living or lower spiritual entities, such as lakes, sea, rocks, or rivers. The creative act of naming calls into being a person who is expected to perform in a given way in society.

The Akan associate surnames with the *ntoro, sunsum,* or *bosom* of the child's father. While there are only seven possible first names for an Akan child, there is an indefinite number of surnames from which a surname can be chosen. However, all surnames are derivable from twelve *abosom* (deities) or *ntoro*. Thus, all names derived from the same *ntoro* or *bosom* are said to possess identical characteristics. The Akan can be classified on the basis of their surnames as members of a particular *bosom* or *ntoro*. This is similar to clan names among other ethnic groups.

There is still another classificatory device for the Akan. For example, if an Akan says *Meye Asonani* (I am a member of the Asona *abusua*), the word *Asonani* identifies him as a member of an ancestral communication community. The principle governing membership of the *abusua* or ancestral communication community is *mogya*, consanguinity.

Akan are classified into political, social, and economic groups on the basis of blood relationships. People who are believed to have identical blood are said to be members of the same *abusua*. To the Akan, *mogya* becomes a person's *saman* (ghost) at his death, retaining a bodily form with a possibility of reincarnation through a female of the same *abusua*.

The *nsamanfo* (the dead) actively participate in the affairs of the *abusua*. The living call on them for guidance in making decisions that affect the members of the *abusua*. The members of the ancestral community are the *euhemeri*, the primal leaders or heroes of the *abusua* system.

The *mogya*, apart from being a psychological state and function, is a fundamental principle for determining membership of the *abusua*. It is the psychological, spiritual, and biological boundary-setting attribute, which includes or excludes people as members or nonmembers. This can be referred to as the principle of consanguinity. Appiah says, "The principle of consanguinity, together with the principles of kra-din and ntoroism or abosomism, constitutes the group inclusion principle that transcends territorial and linguistic considerations."[70]

The Akan believe that the *mogya*, which is both biologically and spiritually conditioned, can only be bestowed by female members of the same *abusua* system. If consanguinity is the only criterion for determining membership of the *abusua*, and if marriage is exogamous, then it is a woman, rather than a man, who can *always* be proven to have identical blood (*mogya*) with the children to whom she gives birth. No one exists as a detached, separate, alienated individual. We are all connected by the generative word.

The *abusua* differs from the family in patrilineal societies, both in size and functions. While a family consists of a husband and wife and their offspring, an *abusua* consists of all people whose blood relation can be traced to a common female ancestor. Indeed, the myth concerning the origin and distribution of Akan *abusua* groups holds that there are seven or eight *abusua* groups, all of which are said to be descended from a common female ancestor. For example, if a person is from the Asona *abusua*, then he must have as his origin the village of Adanse Sebenso and the leader of the group is Kuntun Kununku.

Furthermore, each *abusua* group can be identified on the basis of its *akraboa* or *nkraboa* (symbols). For instance, the symbols of the Asona are the red snake, the white vulture, and the crow.

The *abusua* system is the basis for the communication structure of an Akan village, town, or state (oman). Each village, town, or *oman* is composed of a hierarchy of *abusua* groups. The ruling *abusua* is always referred to as *adehye*. The leader of each *abusua* group is called *abusuapanyin*.

Each *abusua* is a sort of miniature administrative body within the village or town government, and is autonomous in its government of its members. The administration of the *abusua* is by its members, with the *abusuapanyin* as the coordinator. The *abusuapanyin*, who is selected by the members on the basis of one's position in the *abusua* hierarchy and proof of good behavior, is always the eldest son of the eldest female member of the *abusua*. He becomes the leader and custodian of the *abusua* property. Every major *abusua* group has a sacred stool, from which expressive power of the *abusuapanyin* is derived. Sacred stools represent the spirits of all deceased members of the *abusua* and therefore are emblems of communication.

The *okyeame* is the learned orator who holds the keys to

effective communication between the king and the people. One might see the entire architecton of Akan society as based upon communication as a control aspect of group solidarity. However, whether or not the concept of *okyeame* provides an explanatory system for interpersonal communication can be answered only on the basis of an Afrocentric world view. The *okyeame* is engaged in intrapersonal, interpersonal, or public communication when he pours libation to the spirit of the ancestors. He is engaged in an interpersonal communicative act when he acts as the spokesperson for the king. The drummer (*akyeremade*) engages in human communication when he addresses his message to the spirit of the Odum tree or to the spirits of the ancestors. Is the individual engaged in an intrapersonal communicative act when his *okra* inspires him with supernatural insights or when his *okra* links his actions with the supernatural community? How does the *okyeame* maintain the harmonious relationships between people? These questions are often untouched in Western discussions of communication; nevertheless, they cannot be exorcized out of human experience, because they are the African experience in Akan culture. Beyond that fact is the presence in the African culture in the Americas of certain Africanisms. Thus, the point of departure for understanding human communication in Akan society is not only its anthropocentric attributes, based on a particular person's intention to speak, but also the total human experiences within a society. Nothing is separate, isolated, detached.

Towards Concrete Images in Discourse

I have discussed the place of the spoken word, the function of speaker, and the character of the audiences in an African concept of rhetoric. But, one will ask, what is the substance of African public discourse? The questioner who poses such a query would be a Euro-American or a Eurocentric African, exercising the contextual criteria provided by Western thought. To ask, What is the *substance?* is to see a dichotomy between form and substance that does not plague most African thought. Since form and content are *activity, force* unifies what is called form and content in creative expression. The speech is meant to be alive and moving in all of its aspects so that separation of the members becomes impossible, because the creative production is "an experience" or a happening occurring within and outside the speaker's soul. Thus, unlike the Euro-American, the African seeks the totality of an experience, concept, or system. Traditional African society looked for unity of the whole rather than specifics of the whole; such a concentration, which also emphasized synthesis more than analysis, contributed to community stability because considerations in the whole were more productive than considerations in detail. Now it is clear that this has a very real bearing upon the making of a public discourse.

The public discourse convinces an audience not merely through attention to logical substance but through the power to fascinate, to generate creative energy. Yet this does not preclude the materials of composition, or the arrangement and structure of those materials; it simply expresses a belief that when images are arranged according to their power and chosen because of their power, the speaker's ability to convince is greater than if he attempted to employ a formal logic. When a speaker possesses visionary ecstasy, vivid but controlled, his audiences' participation is more assured than if he exercised only syllogistic reasoning. Perhaps that is drawing the choices too sharply, inasmuch as few neo-Aristotelians would argue for a dichotomy of emotion and logic. However, it is necessary to state the polar positions to illustrate the emphasis of the traditional African speaker. The African speaker means to be poet, not lecturer; indeed, the rhythmic equipment of the two will always be different. So now it is possible to say that traditional African public discourse is given to concrete images that are capable of producing compulsive relationships and invoking the inner needs of audiences because of the inherent power of the images. A mastery of proverbs is a good resource for the speaker who invokes tradition. Additionally, the more powerful the speaker, the more fascinated the audiences will be. And power is derived from the experience of the "orality" and spirituality of the presentation.

To maintain that fascination, the African American speaker seeks to appeal to the principal myths. The African, with an unbroken link to the traditions, maintains that linkage organically. For the African American, the task is to find the myths that have developed in our American history. These are the driving forces of our sanity. High John de Conqueror, the Flying African, Shine, John Henry, Stagolee, and others inform the communicative dimension of our lives.

Part 2 **The Resistance**

This section addresses the invention of African American communication—the substance and form of discourse, particularly in its oral dimension, orature. Drawing on African heritage and the unique American experience, the African American community generates myths that enable the understanding of heroic figures who are able to transcend the negative impact of that experience. How the rhetoric of resistance emerged from these myths is a central concern. The making of a discourse that confronts the human condition of oppression has been a principal preoccupation of African American spokespersons.

African American Orature
and Context

The study of African American oratory is intricately inter-
woven with the study of history; and a central aspect of African American history is the persistent public discussions
related to our American experience. Having to defend our humanity, to agitate for minimal rights, and to soothe the raw
emotions of mistreated fellows, our speakers have been forced
to develop articulate and effective speech behavior on the
platform. That a principal dimension of black history is encompassed by platform activities in the form of lectures, sermons, and agitations should stand without question from the
student familiar with history.

Unable to read or write English and forbidden by law (in
most states) to learn, the African in America early cultivated
the natural fascination with *nommo,* the word, and demonstrated a singular appreciation for the subtleties, pleasures,
and potentials of the spoken word, which has continued to en-
rich and embolden his history. Thus, in part because of strict
antiliteracy laws during slavery, vocal communication became, for a much greater proportion of blacks than whites,
the fundamental medium of communication. Orature, the
total oral tradition of Africans and African Americans, provides a comprehensive corpus of work for examination.

Orature is the comprehensive body of oral discourse on every subject and in every genre of expression produced by people of African descent. It includes sermons, lectures, raps, the dozen, poetry, and humor. *Oratory* refers to the practice of eloquent public speaking. One studies oratory by studying speeches—that is, the critique of strengths and weaknesses in a public presentation.

The study of black speeches, then, emphatically imposes itself upon any true investigation into our history and orature. Bringing to America a fertile oral tradition augmented by the pervasiveness of *nommo*, the generating and sustaining powers of the spoken word, orature permeated every department of life.[1] As in African society, so in early African communities in America, disorganized and frustrated by overlordships though they were, the word influenced all activities, all movement in nature. Plantation slaves could look to the firmament and reorder the stars or they could gather to sing away (which is also encompassed in *nommo*) their "trials and tribulations."[2] Everything appears to have rested upon the lifegiving power of the word: life, death, disease, health, and, as the career of Nat Turner demonstrates, even liberation. For the word could not be considered static; it was then and is now dynamic and generative. Actually, this concept embodies the idea of incantation as transformation; vocal expression reigns supreme.

Within this context, the almost methodical pathos of Martin Luther King can be viewed alongside the mournful utterances of Ray Charles; the vocal expressions of both simply reflect different parts of the same theme. Occasionally, expression seems expertly planned to evoke responses, much as a speaker might prepare persuasive arguments with an eye towards a special kind of reaction. At other times expression bursts forth in a "hallelujah," "doing my thing," or the creation of a totally new sound. The sound of words can often assume as much importance as presentation of arguments in such situations. What is at play is far more significant than the proper or correct pronunciation of words or the right use of *chirologia* and *chironomia;* in most cases, the speaker transforms his audience through the spontaneous exaggeration of sounds combined with the presentation of vital themes. This is in some ways analogous to the African view that the power of transformation can never be in things that depend on men to control them, but must reside in *bantu,* or human beings.[3] Argument, because it is formulated and arranged by humans, has no power of itself, except as it is expressed by humans. As a fetish has no power of its own but can only be efficacious when the word is spoken, so the proper expression by the right person of an argument or song may bring results. In this sense, therefore, black gospel preachers and blues singers are sharing in the same experiential spontaneity when they rely on vocal creativity to transform the audience.

With an African heritage steeped in orature and the acceptance of transforming vocal communication, the African American developed a consummate skill in using language to produce communication patterns alternative to those employed in the American situation. These channels remained rhetorical, even as they consciously or subconsciously utilized linguistic changes for communicative effectiveness. During slavery, communication between different ethnic and linguistic groups was difficult, but the almost universal African regard for the power of the spoken word contributed to the development of alternative communication patterns in the work songs, Ebonics, sermons, and the spirituals with their dual meanings, one for the body and one for the soul. It is precisely the power of the word, whether in music or speeches, that authentically speaks of an African heritage.[4] Thus to omit orature as manifest in speeches and songs from any proper investigation of African American history is to ignore the essential ingredient in the making of our drama.

The Power of Nommo

Let us look at this more closely. To understand the nature of African American communication means that one must understand that *nommo* continues to permeate our existence.[5] This is not to say that all or even most of us, given the situation, can immediately identify the transforming power of vocal expression. It is apparent when a person says, "Man, that cat can rap." Or one can identify it through the words of the sister leaving a Baptist church, "I didn't understand all those words the preacher was using, but they sure sounded good." Inasmuch as the *nommo* experience can be found in many aspects of African American life, one can almost think of it as a way of life. Therefore, the scholar, rhetorician, or historian who undertakes an analysis of the black past without recognizing the significance of vocal expression as a transforming agent is treading on intellectual quicksand.

What is clear is that the black leaders who articulated and articulate the grievances felt by the masses have always understood the power of the word in the black community. This is the meaning of the messianism I speak of in regard to Nat Turner, Martin Luther King, and others. Their emergence has always been predicated upon the power of the spoken word. Indeed, it is extremely difficult to speak of black leaders without speaking of spokespersons in the elemental sense, who were vocally brilliant and could move audiences with sudden tears or quick smiles. It is no fluke of history that persons who only had letters after their names or organizational talents have seldom been acclaimed "black leaders"; it is rather a fact, intricately related to the eminence of the spoken word within the black community. The able historian, Carter G. Woodson, understood this most clearly, as indicated in his 1925 work *Negro Orators and Their Orations*.[6] Other black historians have given more than passing attention to the influence of black orators on the black community. In books by Eppse, Quarles, Ferris, and others, significant commentary is devoted to the oratorical gifts of black leaders.[7] Discussing orature therefore becomes, for the serious student of our culture, an attempt to interpret the preeminence of the spoken word.

Slavery and Rhetoric

The central fact of black history in America is slavery and antislavery, which stands astride every meaningful rhetorical pathway like a giant elephant. That black speakers before and after the abolition of slavery are concerned with it is immensely important in the development of eloquence. However, it is not only physical slavery that dominates the history of America but the exploitation of the African through ideological impositions. Europe is insinuated into every aspect of black existence, even the sacred process of naming. Black discourse, therefore, to be healthy discourse, is resistance. While the stated theme of a speech may be white racism, black pride, American hypocrisy, freedom, crime, poverty, desegregation, poor housing conditions, and voting rights, the underlying issue to be dealt with is always the slavery experience. What shall be made of it? How shall we more adequately deal with the residual effects of slavery? And how can we regain our pre-slavery—indeed, pre-American—heritage?

What is more demonstrative of a people's proud heritage than the pre-American values and attitudes of Africans? When the Yoruba, Fanti, Efik, Congo, Asante, Dahomeans, and Mandingo arrived in America, they had no past of family instability, disrespect for elders, and juvenile insurrection. So when the contemporary warrior-orators express the belief that white racism has been the chief obstacle to black psychological and physical liberation, they are speaking of the central position of slavery in our history. They are taking an antiapartheid, antislavery, antiracist position and are becoming in the process the embodiment of the resistance. It is this psychological-political resistance that constitutes a universe of alternative discourse.

As human slavery is the central fact of African history in America, so antislavery is the crucible of black rhetorical expression. Although there had been African protest, vocal and physical, to slavery, a steady stream of orators against slavery did not spring forth until the turn of the nineteenth century. The pressure upon blacks to defend themselves as human beings while agitating for equal rights, combined with the need to correct false and demeaning characterizations of Africans, provided constant practice on the platform. Many of the leading speakers gravitated towards the seminaries, learning the rules of homiletics and exegesis.[8] Once out of school, they often applied practical lessons in public speaking and analysis to their natural gifts and were soon on their way to becoming accomplished orators. Not a few African American speakers learned the rudiments of the "proper rules" of rhetoric from seminary training; others learned from the Quaker abolitionists. All of them used *nommo*, the productive word, to the advantage of their eloquence.

The early African speeches in America dealt with the institution of slavery. By the nineteenth century, Peter Williams, James Forten, and Theodore Wright were using their rhetorical abilities to state grievances and to chart future directions for the race. In 1808, Peter Williams spoke on the "Abolition of the Slave Trade" and expressed hope that Africans would soon be free. But the slave trade continued beyond the constitutional deadline in many instances, like a runner past the designated finish line, and slavery draped its misery more completely over its African subjects. However, Williams' speech expressed the universal optimism of a people who knew that things had to get better, because nothing was more horrible than slavery.

Although black spokespersons have been priests, they have more often been prophets. Subsequent to Williams' 1808 address, other speakers spoke optimistically of deliverance in both a practical and a mystical sense. One might refer to this phenomenon as messianism (as I discuss elsewhere in this volume). Characterized by prophetic visions, it is often present in the rhetoric of oppressed people. The orators voiced their opposition to the oppressing agent and simultaneously looked for some type of manifestation, either in person or process, capable of alleviating their suffering, thereby bringing in the millennium. In their speeches, messianism was manifest on two levels: (1) black salvation and (2) world salvation. Many orators saw the black "saints" liberating the world. The orators, like the poets, spoke of "strong men coming," but unlike the poets, they were often the embodiment of their rhetoric, or at least they and others thought so.[9] When Marcus Garvey stormed out of the West Indies in the first quarter of the twentieth century with his doctrine of psychic and physical migration to Africa, he became the sum total of black salvation to millions.[10] In fact, the psychological implications of the cult orators are that they believe, and their votarists believe them to be, the fulfillment of the rhetoric. One thinks immediately of the language of Daddy Grace: *"The Bible says you shall be saved by Grace, I'm Grace."* Nat Turner saw himself as the vicar of God upon the earth. And in 1914 the mother of Father Divine's church, Lorraine, stood on the grounds of the White House saying, "The Lord has come."

In such a psychological climate, the name Moses grew as important in Africans' minds as the person had been in Israel's eyes, and dominated the future of blacks as Moses had dominated the history of Jews. "Go down, Moses, Way Down in Egypt's Land, Tell Ol' Pharaoh to Let My People Go," was symbolic of the Africans' hope. It was this kind of optimism that had swept over blacks in the North on January 1, 1808, the day slave trading was to be abolished. While the Northern blacks leaped with joy, the Southern whites put sharper thorns under the feet of the slaves. Blacks who were not enslaved could see a new day dawning that had neither the blemish of the trade nor the dark spot of the institution in its horizon, and their speeches reflected this optimism. Williams says:

> *But let us no longer pursue a theme of boundless affliction. An enchanting sound now demands your attention.* Hail! Hail! glorious day, whose resplendent rising disperseth the clouds which have hovered with destruction over the land of Africa, and illumines it by the most brilliant rays of future prosperity. Rejoice, oh! Africans! No longer shall

tyranny, war and injustice, with irresistible sway, deso-
late your native country. Rejoice, my brethren, that the
channels are obstructed through which slavery, and its
direful concomitants, have been entailed on the African
race.[11]

Such optimism is born of a people obsessed with the future,
particularly when the past had been so terrible.

The antislavery speeches of black abolitionists soon came
to have a discernible structure. The rhetor spoke of slavery's
history and horrors, eulogized white philanthropists (mostly
Quakers), and appealed to God for deliverance. Every black
orator knew the institution of slavery from beginning to end,
which was necessary knowledge for public speeches. And
many black speakers worked closely with white philanthropists and abolitionists and therefore could speak easily of
white contributions. The radical Quakers, who were often in
the middle of public discussions on the issue of slavery, en-
deared themselves to black orators. Their exploits became in-
centives for blacks who agitated for the liberation of their enslaved brethren. Actually tailored for the times, the speeches
almost always ended with some method of mythication.[12]
Invocations, poems, and religious expressions, calling on God
to intervene in one way or another, were prevalent in the
speeches of black antislavery orators. Thus the black antislavery speakers contributed to the heightening of contradictions
within the pre–Civil War American society by constant use of
religious symbolism to express their position and their re-
definition of cultural heroes by honoring white abolitionists.
A Eurocentric critique of the discourse of this period often
casts the black speakers in the role of reactionaries when, in
fact, they often defined the grounds of discourse.

After the Civil War, vocal expression did even more to mold
the ideas of Afro-Americans who could now assemble with
relative ease. Their heroes and heroines were antislavery
fighters, midnight runners, and underground railroad "con-
ductors." Although laws were quickly enacted against loiter-
ing, black religious assemblies were permitted and several ca-

pable speakers appeared between 1865 and 1920 with various proposals and programs for black salvation. But of the parade of "orators" who marched across the stage in full view of the destitute black masses, Marcus Garvey possessed an awesome combination of force and form to electrify millions. His bombastic oratorical performances, played out with sensitive and dramatic understanding of a cultural phenomenon, made him the most widely acclaimed black spokesman of any generation. From Garvey's time onward, black oratory would simultaneously contain something of his political and social opinion as well as a portion of his cultural and ethnic responsiveness. Garvey drummed his message to the quickening intellectual and emotional pace of the African audience. Democracy and freedom were in the air and the rhythm of the time was: Wake up, black man!

Despite this fact, the extensive implications of *nommo* are not clearly sensed in sole concentration on the political and social rhetoric of Afro-Americans. Probably only within the religious experience, when worshippers and leaders—including preachers, deacons, and church mothers—interact, does the concept blossom into its full communicative significance. The complexities of the religious interactive event, which can involve from one person responding to a preacher to nearly the whole congregation caught up in continuous response, ranging from weeping to shouts of joy, are indicative of the several interlocking communication networks that may be set off when the preacher gives the word.

Such response configurations are not begun automatically; every speaker does not possess the assurance that he will be successful in provoking a total response. In fact, some preachers never succeed in moving an audience to the total interactive event, which is necessary for them to consider their speeches successful. These preachers must be satisfied with the occasional feedback expressed by an "Amen" or a "Lord, help," offered by several members as the sermon is presented. Other preachers, through a delicate combination of vocal manipulations, characterized by rhythm and cadence, and vital thematic expression, usually developed in narrative form, can

easily produce a creative environment when message is inten-
sified by audience response.

Understanding the oral emphasis within the traditional African American churches, one becomes aware of the close relationship between speech and music. The antiphonal pattern, where the speaker presents a theme that is answered by
respondents, pervades our speech as it permeates African
music. Writing of the relationship of African music to Afro-
American music in *Blues People,* LeRoi Jones (Amiri Baraka)
observes: "The most salient characteristics of African, or at
least West African, music is a type of song in which there is a
leader and a chorus; the leading lines are sung by a single
voice, the leader's, alternating with a refrain sung by the
chorus."[13] While this pattern in music may be African in origin, it is not uncommon to Afro-American religious singing.
The leader "lines" the song and the congregation responds,
thus fulfilling the *antiphony.*

Speech and music, as manifestations of *nommo,* relate in
still another manner within black churches. As mentioned
earlier, a speaker is not assured of a totally interactive audience unless he blends the proper vocal rhythms and thematic
interests. In addition to these elements, the communicative
situation can be made more productive by audience condi-
tioning through singing. In this sense, singing sets the stage
or mood by preparing the audience emotionally and physi-
cally for the preacher, whose communication task is made
easier because of the audience receptivity. Singing, then, in
the black religious audience, although instructive, is much
more palliative; it soothes the emotions and draws the congregation together. Not having to concentrate on rhetorical
means to encourage cohesiveness, the preacher inherits an
attentive audience by virtue of the choir's work. In mount-
ing the platform to speak to a religious audience, the black
preacher does not challenge *nommo* but uses it, becomes a
part of it, and is consumed in the fire of speech and music. The
perfect force of the moment is sensual, giving, sharing, generative, productive, and ultimately creative and full of power.
Hallelujah!

The sermon, as the principal spoken discourse during the religious service, can reflect the preacher's awareness of the audience's responsiveness. His voice proves extremely significant as he alternates stressed and unstressed syllables, giving even the pauses rhythmic qualities. Witnessing the mixed outpouring of breathing and syllabic patterns, it is clear to the observer that the preacher initiates and sustains a tension between an audience and himself through vocal expression. The basic vocal pattern is established by the preacher and is accompanied by a secondary pattern emanating from the audience. Thus the spoken word, as a sermon, appears to maintain the essential unity of the interlocking communication networks in its role as the main event of the religious service.

The socio-historical perspectives of black orature, whether African or American based, share certain common grounds. Central to the understanding of the role of vocal expressiveness within the African American community are *nommo*, the generative and dynamic quality of vocal expression, and slavery, the primary fact of black existence in America. *Nommo* has continued to manifest itself in the black community, notably within the church; and slavery's role in American history, while providing a common reference point, has made all black speeches relative. Historically, black oratory, both sacred and secular, has been collective in the same sense that most artistic productions are created for and meant to be shared by entire audiences. To understand the nature of discourse in the African American community, we should examine African conceptions of communication, inasmuch as the connection has been well established.

The philosophical basis of communication in Africa was celebrated in the West when Father Placied Tempels, a Belgian monk whose first language was Flemish, published *Bantoe-Filosofie* in 1945 and in 1946 brought out the French edition. In 1956, this work was translated into German and then became available to a wide European audience. What makes Tempels' work important is the fact that, as a Franciscan missionary in the Congo (now Zaire) since 1933, he had meticulously recorded his observations of the Baluba people. His presentation of Baluba thought as an integrated system of philosophy provided a refreshing portrait of the complexity of African thought.

Marcel Griaule's research among the Dogon people of Mali was published in 1947. Griaule, an ethnologist, had spent years studying the behaviors, social and economic, of the Dogon. His interest in their metaphysical system led him to seek out a great priest and hunter named Ogotommêli. In October 1946, Ogotommêli, who had been accidentally blinded, summoned Griaule to his house for a conversation on Dogon philosophy. For thirty-three days, Ogotommêli expounded to Griaule the world system, the religion, the metaphysics, and ethics of the Dogon people, invalidating many of the negative conceptions of Europeans held about African genius. Ogotommêli's language was elaborate, symbolic, and eloquent. His images were full and his meanings precise. Griaule recorded Ogotommêli's conversations in the Dogon language and translated them into French, then published a book (translated in English) as *Conversations with Ogotommêli*.[14]

The significance of Griaule's interaction with the Dogon is that he became a student. Marcel Griaule, anthropologist, found that it took sixteen years of meetings and discussions with the Dogon before he could understand the abstract knowledge eventually presented to him. Indeed, there are four stages to knowledge in Dogon culture: (1) the word at face value, (2) the word off to the side, (3) the word from behind, and (4) the clear word. The eight levels of the clear word are reserved for the highest priests who have shown evidence of many years of study. Griaule reached only the first level of the clear word!

A collaborator and colleague of Griaule, Germaine Dieterlen, worked among the Bambara, neighbors of the Dogon, to produce "An Essay on Bambara Religion." Of course, Rattray had done work in English on the Asante (Ashanti), and the Yoruba had been studied by both British and Yoruba scholars, but the intense interest produced by Tempels' and Griaule's books reasserted the philosophical richness of African thought for the European mind.

African American thought, as expressed in religion and myth, may be seen as an extension of the African foundations. Paul Carter Harrison writes in *The Drama of Nommo* that even "the popular dance of African/Americans is a continuation of the African sensibility."[15] African American spoken discourse continues the sensibilities expressed as orature on the continent. Oswald Spengler once wrote of the African as demonstrating "not a purposed organization of space such as we find in the mosque and the cathedral, but a rhythmically ordered sequence of spaces."[16] While it is often difficult to tell what Spengler thought of the "rhythmically ordered sequence of spaces" that constitutes the African frame of mind, clearly he understood, even in his unwillingness to appreciate the richness of the African culture, that its rhythms were different. In the movements and spaces, the circles and curves, and the artistic sensibilities of the ancient traditions, one still finds the allegiance to transcending rhythms.

Mythoforms in African American Communication

Myth, conventionally defined as a traditional story or tale that has functional value for a society, usually serves as a way of dealing with mystery. For example, all known cultures have creation myths that relate humans to nature, explaining where we came from and where we are going. In the modern Western world, myth has become synonymous with fallacy and superstition and is associated with an escape from, rather than an immersion in, reality—its original purpose.[17] In industrialized societies, science denies mystery and technology replaces mythmaking. In the information age, Western culture is intent on demystification and deconstruction. But while science and technology seem to have answered some basic questions about life on the planet, they have also contributed greatly to human uncertainty. Anxiety, accompanying the possibility of nuclear holocaust, mars children's lives and Western technological society lacks the words with which to build an interposing myth.

Lévi-Strauss claims that myths operate without our knowledge.[18] In conventional thinking, a myth is normally considered a story or tale of a traditional nature that has functional value for a society. However, *mythos*, the Greek word from which we derive "myth," actually meant "utterance." When *mythos* was connected to *logos*, "the study of," we were able to achieve *mytho-logia*, "mythology," the study of myth or analytical utterance. So it is precisely because these "deep utterances" operate at unconscious levels that they maintain our symbolic life at a conscious level.

We are no longer victims of an alien nature that threatens to subdue us; we are, as the continental Africans would teach us, structured by the symbol, *nommo*, that makes us one with nature. In the mind of the African sages, we are of the same essence as the cells of trees and plants. We are, quite honestly, not humans separated from other matter; we are, more correctly, as the physicists now understand, of the same nature. Within this context, myth is an organizing principle in human symbolic discourse. What is it that we speak of if it is not life or death?

Myth is most pervasive as a mythoform, the all-encompassing deep generator of ideas and concepts in our living relationship with our peers, friends, and ancestors. A productive force, it creates discourse forms that enable speakers to use cultural sources effectively. Mythoform is different from the universal principle that Armstrong seeks by an exposition of the creative works of Yoruba artists.[19] I am not convinced that what he seeks exists. He is correct to challenge Jung, Lévi-Strauss, and others for exalting Western cultural concepts to universality, but Armstrong overreacts by seeking the underlying patterns that give rise to all of the myths of all cultures. This is unnecessary and indeed impossible, unless of course one sees life itself as the essential generator, the mythoform, for all concepts.

The Nigerian critic and theorist of myth, Isidore Okpewho, attempts to set the Ijo creation myth of Woyengi within its context, only to be beguiled by the overarching symbolism of Lévi-Strauss.[20] Okpewho chooses to use Lévi-Strauss as a starting point for his critique of the Woyengi myth, without consideration of the sharp criticism of Lévi-Strauss by Armstrong. This is unfortunate, because he falls completely into the Western structuralist trap, which gives him no way to escape. Okpewho is directed by the same "constraining structures of the mind" that he found in Lévi-Strauss.[21] Thus, he writes that he will try to discover "by means of structural analysis and the aid of ethnographic inquiry, the informing matrix of thought and concern in the tale."[22] What he discovers, in spite of his structuralist endeavor with the Woyengi tale and his rather acerbic aside against the position of Cheikh Anta Diop on the place of matriarchy in Africa, is that static structuralism, tied to Western frames, cannot inform dynamic, polyvalent mythic possibilities that are meta-Western. Between the beginning of consciousness and the unknown is a great amount of human philosophical discussion and activity about the prior-to-consciousness and the after-consciousness; rhetoric is therefore the discussion of life and death, consciousness and unconsciousness, being and nonbeing. Every act that exists in the realms of deliberation, forensics, or panegyrics is an act in the conscious. To act philosophically is to act mythologically. Rhetoric becomes mythological action when it considers the prior-to and the after-consciousness, even while they occur in consciousness.

African American Mythmaking

These analytical utterances, or rather utterances with imbedded messages, can be found in most contemporary speeches of African Americans. In the most passionate rhetoric and actions of African Americans we still find that *pathos* accompanies *mythos* into the twentieth century. Therefore, a discussion of the nature of myth in African American thought is a way to discover the values of a spiritual, traditional, even mystical rhetoric as it confronts a technological, linear world and to provide us with ideas for an Afrocentric alternative to apocalyptic thinking. I have chosen to consider the evidence of African American culture alone, an Afrocentric view, to say that the context of the mythoform is such that it adapts to the circumstances of history. In this respect, the myths I examine have nothing to do with the general concept of universality. They represent the African's response in the Americas to a historical moment. (Now it is true that other cultures have similar responses to similar conditions, but these must be seen in their own, fundamental contexts.) The utterances are not mythoforms themselves; they are only enactments of the mythoforms. Thus, mythoforms are the basal psychic patterns by which we organize our experiences. These are reported in various existential enactments.

In the language of the African American speaker, myth becomes an explanation for the human condition and an answer to the problem of psychological existence in a racist society. This is not different from the myths of Oduduwa among the Yoruba or Okomfo Anokye among the Asante—or a hundred other African ethnic communities. Creation myths of the type found in traditional African and European cultures are not present in the African American cultural experience, if we take the formal arrival of Africans in the Virginia colony in 1619 as a point of departure. The creation myths of Africa remained intact for most Africans, and therefore the practical myths dealt with questions of geographical and cultural alienation, conflict with a hostile society, and the separation of technology and nature. What is more significant is that myth is connected to life and its social functions. Relationships between family members and relationships to outsiders are at the heart of a functional doctrine of the myth. We act mythically. But functionalism alone cannot dictate what myth is or should be. How can a mythoform be used?

One use of mythoforms is to preserve links to the past—that is, a cultural history. Let us be clear that we understand the ever-presence of the ancestors. When we speak of the African community, we are speaking of the *living* and the *dead*. Recall the earlier explanations of the nature of libation among the Ga celebrations of community throughout African societies, and of *nommo* as a collective experience; in fact, without the participation of the ancestors, *nommo* cannot be completed since the dead are the agents who continue to energize the living. They assure us that the discourse of life will not be chaotic, and we take this, in whatever society we live, as a permanent expression of rebirth. Perhaps the African American version is truncated by Christianity or Islam or some other non-African mythic expression, but even in modified form we see how ancestral myths are a part of our communicative sense.

The ability to recognize ancestral myths is often left to the older members of the black community. They recall the traditional songs and the oral reports that refer to certain myths imbedded in verbal expressions. For example, the admonition frequently heard in south Georgia, "Call me like you gon' call me when I am dead," had as much imbedded continuity as the passed-down banjo or the hot irons used to press clothes. The elders find a connectedness with their past when they hear such a direct reference to the adoration given to the dead. However, beyond what appears to be a metaphysical attachment is the continuation of practices that find their source in the traditions.

The work of Melville Herskovits in *The Myth of the Negro Past* still stands as a monument to the powerful presence of the African ancestors in the Americas.[23] What Herskovits and others have demonstrated is the abundance of cultural memory in African American societies. Indeed, the ghost tales are often nothing more than the modification of ancestor tales and relate to the near as well as remote past. As a child in Georgia, I often heard my relatives speak of "seeing" great-grandfather or great-grandmother. The folklore often gives the stories to us with expressions such as "This actually happened," "Use to be years ago when we first come here," "Way back there in them days gone by," "This man I know, he was an old, old man," or "My grandpa once told me that he seed his daddy."

Various manifestations of the role of ancestors have occurred in African American society, and there have been special observances at cemeteries where certain types of material possessions have been placed on the graves to appease the ancestors. Libations are still poured in some places in the American South as an indication of respect for "those who are not with us," and despite the Christian religion, much of African American religion is devoted to the idea of transition from life to death to life eternal. "Life eternal" has a special ring to believers because it is easily connected to the belief in reincarnation, the ever-presence of dead spirits, and the fact that the dead are often reborn in the children. We use these concepts as anchors for the mythoforms, or rather the mythoforms find their materiality in the relationship to ancestors.

When we examine the nature and utility of myth in African American discourse, we see that it is about ancestral heroes and heroines. The African American myth is the highest order of symbolic motifs. Furthermore, the myth emerges as a story with a basis in historical or indefinite time, but in all cases the story is of triumphs and victories, even if it is considered in the suffering-myth genre or is found in Ananse- or Brer Rabbit–type tales.

A significant function of the African American myth in discourse is the demonstration of control over circumstances, as opposed to control over nature. It is the heroine's or hero's mission, sometimes messianic in nature, to surmount any obstacle in the cause of peace, love, or collective harmony. African American myths are set in the inexact past—unless, of course, they are historic, legendary myths, such as Harriet Tubman's. In such cases they are set in a specific time and place, although they may be of anonymous origin. If we use Stagolee, John Henry, Harriet Tubman, Shine, or John Jasper as examples of some African American myths, we can see how myth also functions as a proto-science. It can provide solutions to crises in the collective life of the people. In this way it is not aetiological—that is, merely offering causes for conditions and circumstances—but rather poignantly eschatological. What we notice when we examine African American myths is that they possess a kind of epistemological maturity, unlike the traditional African myth, which may be seen as an interpretation of reality. The idea of hope and possibility rises on the shoulders of an African American imaginative mythology that sees the future as brighter than the present. Social situations molded the ultimate form of this myth. A story may demonstrate the myth but is not the myth.

Hope is typified in the mythological character called Shine. This version of the ballad appeared in Georgia in the 1950s:

> Shine, little Harlem boy blacker than me,
> Sailed the wrong ship in the wrong sea.
> Old *Titanic* hit a iceberg block,
> Shook and shimmied and reared from shock.
> Shine come up from the engine floor
> Running so fast he broke down an iron door.
> Captain told Shine, "Get on back downstairs!"
> Shine told the Captain, "You better say your prayers."
> Captain's daughter hollered, "Lord, the water's up to my
>   neck."
> Shine said, "Baby you'd better swim, by heck."
> Captain said, "Boy I got pumps to pump the water
>   down."
> Shine said, "Pump on, I want be around."
> Shine jumped overboard into the sea
> Looked back at the white folks and said, "Swim like
>   me."
> And he swam on.
> Captain's daughter hist her dress over her head
> Shine said, "You'll catch pneumonia baby and be stone
>   cold dead."

And he swam on.
Captain's daughter cried, "Shine, Shine, save poor me
and I'll give everything your eyes can see."
Shine said, "There's plenty on land baby, waiting for
  me."
And he swam on.
Captain yelled, "Shine, my boy, I got a bank account.
Save poor me and you'll get any amount."
Shine said, "More banks on land than on sea."
And he swam on.
White headed millionaire, aged eighty five,
Titanic deck yelling, "I want to stay alive.
Shine, Shine, hear my plea!"
Shine said, "Jump in the sea Grandpa, and swim like
  me."
And Shine swam on.
Five o'clock in the morning in Harlem and daybreak
  near.
Shine said, "How come they close up these bars so
early when Shine just got here?"
And he walked on.
Newsstand on the corner, bought the *Daily News*.
Nothing on the front page but *Titanic* blues.
He walked on.
Got to his girl friend's house,
She cried, "How can it be?"
Shine said, "Yes baby it's me."
And they got it on.

"Shine" is preeminently a myth of self-discovery in the midst
of chaos. This is one of the moments of crisis that African
American mythic figures like to enter. Harriet Tubman, with
slavery and human bondage; John Henry, with the challenge
of a mountain; High John de Conquerer, with any and every
conceivable personal difficulty; and Shine, with the sinking of
the *Titanic*, are self-discovery myths.

Melvin Dixon writes that "the moment of self-discovery has

been one of the more dramatic turning points in the personal history of every black American."[25] In the moment of crisis, Shine recognizes that his condition was normally one of second-class status but that *he* could swim. This discovery gives him power over the white and wealthy that he would never have achieved if it had not been for the sinking of the *Titanic*. The moral is not lost on the African American community: Crisis has a way of equalizing everyone.

There are some aspects to the use of myths in African American discourse that are filled with slaveship pathos. The fact that myth functions means only that it is recognized as having certain positive capabilities, and the managing of myths in discourse could lead to a renewed emphasis on deep style in orature and, quite correctly, introduce another uniquely African American element on the public platform. Contemporary African American myth contains the powerful suffering genre. Even in the most victorious myths, one frequently finds the suffering genre. Perhaps this is because victory, in a political sense, is often based upon suffering in the minds of African Americans. How to turn the suffering genre into a positive, victorious consciousness occupies a whole Afrocentric literary school of thought.

Baldwin and Richards have written extensively on the cultural question, with direct reference to the crisis in African American motifs.[26] Baldwin sees the psychology of oppression as giving birth to the complex mental confusion besetting the African American. On the other hand, Richards, after Karenga and Diop, has analyzed the extent of the cultural malady that afflicts a whole generation of thinkers and artists incapsulated by European cultural domination. Out of the cauldron has come the suffering genre in African American myths. There is an implicit belief that suffering brings redemption. In fact, it is the peculiarly African American emphasis, similar to the Christian myth, that gives its potency in contemporary society. Black speakers have frequently allied themselves (or the masses) with this suffering Christ, who would save humanity. In the speeches of Booker T. Washington one can see the myth of suffering redemption at work: God has a great purpose for a people whom he allowed to suffer so much. Like Jesus Christ, the African race was going through the Valley of the Shadow of Death to rise again at the new dawn, having saved the world through its substantive, creative experience of pain.

Akin to the suffering genre is the suckling genre, mainly (but not entirely) identified with the mother-earth, which relates everything to the motif of caring. We care for the world, not just for our own children, and in our myth the suckling mother is a multimammarian who gives milk to all, equally. Our speakers speak of "the brotherhood of man and the fatherhood of God" and move on to illustrate that if God will not take care of others, then our mothers will mop the sweat off the brows of all. Martin Luther King Jr. called such individuals "men and women who will be as maladjusted as the prophet Amos, who in the midst of the injustices of his day would cry out in words that echo across the centuries, 'Let justice roll down like waters, and righteousness like a mighty stream.'"[27] Nearly seventy-five years earlier, Joseph C. Price, the outstanding orator and educator of the nineteenth century, had said, "There is no true freedom that does not give full recognition and assent to that cardinal principle of humanity—the fatherhood of God and the brotherhood of man."[28] In many respects, the suckling myth establishes the African American as responsible for the world. Somehow we will purge the world of its sins through our suffering; we will teach the brotherhood and sisterhood of the earth. This becomes a suckling mythology, as befits a redemptive or messianic idea.

Harriet Tubman is a extraordinary mythic figure in our rhetorical consciousness because she is symbolic, that is, an expression of our epic journey. Tubman's transformation from birth to self-imposed exile, to rites of initiation, to triumphant return to the South to deliver her brothers and sisters represents all of us. In that sense, she is more than symbol, she is enactment. Within the African American cosmos, Tubman is a combination of intense secular and sacred power. She established her credibility; that is, she became a heroic character by carrying out her professed actions. The deliverance of more than three hundred slaves from bondage during the most difficult period of slavery indelibly wrote her name in the mythology of African American discourse. Children are often taught to sing "I love Harriet Tubman because she first loved me." Tubman embodies the care and concern of a mother figure; she is the Great Mother.

She is also what Armstrong calls an "affecting presence," because her enactments occur in a special way: "by presentation and celebration, the existential and generative germ of the culture."[29] We call her name in the secret hours of the night when we lay our children down to sleep, when we fly in airplanes over the seas, when we reach into our psychic lives for strength to overcome stress, when we seek guidance and courage. Armstrong declares that "this is why the affecting presence in all cultures is sometimes venerated, sometimes credited with the power to work good or evil, and is nearly universally valued greatly and accorded distinctive treatment."[30] Tubman is the embodiment, even in her death-life, of a cultural principle, a myth, without precise substance, but a pattern, an enactment of history, profound in its impact upon a community that has known significant epic journeys.

This pattern occurs every time one person reaches back to bring another alongside. Within the Afrocentric culture one sees a distaste for individual achievement that is not related to collective advancement. Harriet Tubman's classic historical action becomes the mythoform for all such patterns of behavior. Any analysis of African American culture must consider the caring mythoform represented in the Tubman example as a possible pattern of behavior. We are confronted by it in the daily interactions of our lives, from the extended-family philosophy to the assistance to the needy in our churches. How can you be well to do and not care about the poor around you? is a particularly Tubman mythoform question. She is heroine, not as an individual, but as a caring, assisting person.

The hero myths that occupy significant places in the African American mythology are, as we've said, John Henry, Stagolee, Shine, John Jasper, Harriet Tubman, and a host of religiously related myths, such as the story of Job. They are hero- or heroine-centered myths because they extend the ordinary to the totality of our cultural existence. John Henry is the strong, powerful steel driver who is capable of drilling a tunnel through a mountain quicker and cleaner than power-driven drills. His ability to use muscle power and physical stamina to overcome the mountain is indicative of the deep reality of the African American's reliance on physical strength during the epic sojourn in America. Use of the John Henry myth is usually confined to instances of physical confrontation or maintenance of philosophical positions. There are instances when the John Henry myth shares some of the characteristics of the Stagolee myth; this is true mainly as each myth regards physical prowess.

Stagolee is the radical impulse to challenge an authority that seeks to repress freedom, improvisation, and harmony. The direct-action orientation of Stagolee is found in Marcus Garvey, Fannie Lou Hamer, Malcolm X, and Martin Luther King Jr. But Stagolee does not have King's religious emphasis; he is a symbol of uncensored, unselfconscious force, pulsating with unpredictability. This mythoform is a recurring pattern in every aspect of African culture in America. The musician who improvises, the basketball player who follows his own rhythms to demonstrate his skill, or the maverick who refuses to have her art suppressed; these are the heroes of the cultural pattern.

Stagolee was the prototype bad man in the sense that nobody bothered him, not even the devil. He is the embodiment of a myth that emphasizes toughness. Known for his supranatural skill at surviving the worst personal tragedy and emerging victoriously, Stagolee is the ultimate projection of the black phallus into the white belly of America. The myth's persistence within the African American community is testimony to its appealing characteristics. What is especially interesting is that Stagolee, unlike John Henry, does not represent the Protestant ethic. John Henry is perceived as the good man who works hard to achieve victory through sweat. Stagolee is his opposite, who will achieve victory by any means necessary. Both are authentic myths of the African American experience and both represent specific characters in the historical and contemporary community; Stagolee, however, retains the fundamental attitude of resistance of the slave revolts.

Stagolee, the representative enactment of the deep-seated and strongly felt sentiment for justice and emancipation, is widely believed by African Americans to be the thorn in the side of a white, hypocritical government. Out of this intellectual and social context is born a manchild in the promised land, as Claude Brown saw it, or a Malcolm X, who preached acid theses, asserted without compromise, against the flailing and anguished figure of an insane political society. As John Illo says, "Indirection is not workable, for the state has stolen irony; satire is futile, its only resource is to repeat the language of the administration."³¹ Only then must the Stagolee myth step forward to demonstrate again how alien we are in this culture and society. But Stagolee is only a presentation, a presence, an enactment, often made symbolic, of the uniqueness that is our experience in America. Such a position in society invites defiance and resistance. In *Die, Nigger, Die,* H. Rap Brown said that when whites say talk low, African Americans should say talk loud; when they say don't play the radio, then play it.³² Brown's reasoning during the Ebony Explosion of the 1960s was that whites tended to disregard the premises of African American discourse and, consequently, did not deserve to have their way, particularly since what they wanted was often contrary to our natural response to the environment. Similarly, the intellectual posture of the black scholar or orator is often based on the attitude of rebellion.

The artist or speaker who uses these myths may never call explicitly upon the names John Henry or Stagolee to express the truth of the myth. However, the myth is so implicit in the culture that its use is impossible to avoid if one engages in any type of discourse. The real mythical essence of these heroes occurs with regularity in the discourse of the African American orator. For example, it was to Stagolee that Robert C. Weaver, former Secretary of Housing and Urban Development in the United States, referred when he said in a speech before the challenge to Democracy of the Fund for the Republic Symposium (June 13, 1963) that "Negroes who are constantly confronted or threatened by discrimination and inequality articulate a sense of outrage. Many react with hostility, sometimes translating their feelings into antisocial actions." Weaver's use of the Stagolee complex was perfect for delivery to a largely white audience, for it did not explain anything about the will of blacks to change the conditions. It was wild, outrageous, hostile, and antisocial behavior in response to a more calculated, wilder, more hostile, and more outrageous discrimination. Weaver knew the Stagolee myth so deeply in his soul that he was able to frame his mouth to say that, in some parts of the community, "a separate culture with deviant values develops." [33] Weaver was talking Stagolee; everything he said described a mythoform well known in the black community, and it was presented by Weaver to his white audience as an explanation of our militant side. Although Weaver used the pejorative language of the white culture to speak of us, he spoke from the deep wellspring of African American historical experiences. To understand Weaver's blacks who "articulate a sense of outrage" is to touch the very source of Stagolee's power. Stagolee is not just bitter; he is outraged at discrimination, paternalism, and bigotry. Thus, when Robert Weaver used the "sense of outrage" term, he was speaking the language of a black community become Stagolee.

Stagolee is the myth that allows the African American to rail against evil with violence, to shoot, to cut, to maim, to kill—if that is necessary to restore a sense of human dignity. Thus, any speaker who uses the appeal to Stagolee, directly or indirectly, is addressing one of the principal hero myths of the community. A classic use of the myth was in Malcolm X's "Black Revolution" speech. In 1964, before a packed crowd at the Militant Labor Forum in New York City, Malcolm said that "you've got 22,000,000 black people in this country today . . . who are fed up with taxation without representation, who are ready to do the same thing your forefathers did to bring about independence."[34] Much of Malcolm X's image as a dynamic orator came from his embodiment of the Stagolee myth in his oratory, and not so much in his personal history. Before his conversion to the teachings of the Honorable Elijah Muhammad, he may have been the personification of Stagolee. However, as a Muslim minister, he was righteous and rather conservative in habits; it was his oratory that carried the Stagolee myth to its highest degree. Malcolm talked outrage and the possibility of violence in the defense of his dignity.

To get beyond the notions of myth as legends of gods, esoteric themes, and aetiological tales, I chose to demonstrate how certain cultural-specific forms are enacted through living celebrations and presentations of being in everyday African American life. Quite frankly, I am not sure one can understand concrete discourse without an appreciation of mythoforms. When I spoke of Harriet Tubman, I mentioned that she was an enactment of our epic journey. I think, however, her historical nature ought to be made plain. In this way we neither confuse history with myth nor myth with specific enactments of mythoforms.

Harriet Tubman is not typical as an expression of myth since she is a legendary but historical mythical character; I mean that there are historical records to attest to her life. Nevertheless, she is perhaps the most salient mythical character in African American history. It is from her that we get the numerous leaders who arise to deliver the people from bondage to salvation. She is not messianic in either the sense of Moses of the Old Testament or Jesus of the New; she is, rather, the spirit-mother, protecting, suckling, and leading her children. The Harriet Tubman enactment of the salvation myth manifests itself in how we relate the stories of the Bible to our everyday realities. Those stories are not real because of the lives of Moses and Jesus; they are real because the experience of Harriet Tubman lives within the hearts of every African American person. That is why people find it difficult to accept the appellation "Moses of her people" for her. She was more than Moses; she was life and love. She performed not out of duty to her people but out of love for them. This is the myth that is found in much of the language of Martin Luther King Jr. In the "Eulogy to Dr. King," Benjamin Mays, himself a celebrated orator, said that there was no element of compulsion in the dying of Martin Luther King. "He was acting on an inner urge that drove him on, more courageous than those who advocate violence as a way out, for they carry weapons of destruction for defence." [35] Not in his nonviolence was King in keeping with Harriet Tubman, but in the "inner urge" to deliver the people. According to the Tubman presentation, she once told a slave who was reluctant to escape, "I'll see you buried and in your grave before I'll see you a slave." Needless to say, the man followed her to freedom.

Myth in its artistic frame and in its Afrocentric reinterpretation elevates and sustains African American culture. Ultimately, Stagolee must be seen as the oratorical or verbal symbol of resistance. We seek to effect the great opposition in discourse by calling upon this major mythoform. Stagolee is an archetype of the rebel, the protest speaker, the revolutionary. And Stagolee, as I shall now discuss, is indeed the discourse metaphor for the rhetoric of resistance.

Rhetoric of Resistance

We invent out of the substance of our culture and from nothing else. If by accident we create something—say, a discourse— then it is not truly invented and not a matter of rhetoric. As a creation, my discourse is new, derived from substances organized in a novel way. A protest speaker, therefore, originates the protest universe of discourse from the unique cultural conditions accompanying the state of oppression or denial that gives birth to the protest in the first place. Bettinghaus perceptively wrote that "when audiences of particular ethnic characteristics are exposed to messages, their responses will be determined in part by the characteristic experiences which they share with other members of the group and for which they have developed particular frames of references."[36]

The African American protest speaker, or writer, is in the employ of a determinism defined by the possibilities and complexities of social protest within a larger society, and is further constricted by the peculiarity of the black experience. As a protest speaker, he is met with the limitations placed upon all protest speakers, but because he is black, a further constraint, based upon socio-historical factors, exists. What rhetorical materials he chooses as a rhetor—in fact, the available materials—are limited, and making-do or creating with the strategies and alternatives prescribed by the social conditions is the real challenge to the African American rhetor. Choosing materials, then, is fundamentally a question of rhetorical invention because it deals with the coming to be of the novel.

If you take the example of the African American poet Aimé Césaire from Martinique, you will see that even in the West Indian response to cultural domination the black speaker or writer must function similarly to the black in the United States. In his great poem, "Return to My Native Country," the indignation of the Martinican condition finally explodes into open revolt and fierce determination to assert a new life.[37] This was a rebellion of language, of symbol, of his entire behavior towards domination. What Césaire chose from the available materials dictated the overthrow of language that was imposed upon him. How Césaire responded to the substance of his condition showed him to be one of the finest modern poets. The spiritual distress that settled over France after the first mass carnage of Europeans at the turn of the century, the racial discrimination practiced by the French in the Caribbean, and the economic crisis in Europe called into question the old values, as well as the place of Africans in colonial territories. Du Bois and Sylvester Williams had begun pan-African conferences, Price-Mars had founded the Haitian Indigenist Movement, Harlem had a renaissance, and in France, Leopold Senghor, Leon Damas, and Aimé Césaire started with what they had available and created the Negritude Movement. This is the circumstance of Césaire's creativity.

Restraints and Rebellions

We expect the frame of reference for the new, the innovative, will always come from African American lifestyles and interactive experiences. How are available resources related to the proposed *invented thing?* While avoiding a detailed classificatory scheme (and, it is hoped, fragmentation), it is possible for us to speak of general bodies of materials that are indispensable to the speaker: *uses and usages of words, prevailing behaviors,* and *"hearerships."*

Theoretically, all of the words in the world are available for the speaker, who can choose among them as they are needed; in reality, however, no speaker has actual access to all the uses and usages of all the possible words. An American speaker, black or white, will certainly choose to speak to American English audiences, unless there are special demands for the occasion; and even so, he might be limited by his knowledge of the language. Therefore, the speaker will make use of words that are accessible to him and to the majority of his audiences.

In addition to language, protest speakers have access to prevailing behaviors, the characteristic rhetor actions (physical and verbal) of a certain culture, which perhaps are even defined by the rhetoricians of that cultural era. Some gestures, mannerisms, and language usages are satisfactorily employed, and are in vogue at one time and place and not at another. Mass media have made the prevailing behaviors culturally available to most rhetors and audiences. While all speakers have theoretical, if not actual, access to the prevailing behaviors of a culture, accessibility, theoretical or actual, does not mean acceptability for those who choose not to employ the prevailing behavior.

Another general category of resources is *hearerships:* collections or gatherings of persons who maintain, if only for the duration of the speech occasion, a special relationship with each other, if only the hearing of a speaker. This is not the place to explore the advantages of this concept over that of audience; suffice it to say that the concept of *hearership* includes a horizontal as well as vertical relationship between hearer and speaker. Hearerships can be available materials for the speakers who can choose the audiences he or she will address. By addressing some at the expense of others, he or she may significantly alter the outcome of the speech. Thus, choosing audiences is as creative a task as choosing what to say; and in persuasive cases, the one is assisted by the other.

What has been outlined are categories common to most speakers, inasmuch as the use of words, prevailing behaviors, and hearerships are available to all speakers. However, *how* the speaker chooses and *what* he chooses are matters of *what* it is possible for him to choose. Consequently, some positions, tactics, and usages are considered off limits by a black protest speaker that are not restrictive for other speakers, black or white.

The speaker is also constrained, in a unique manner, by circumstances, audiences, and personal attributes. The distinctiveness of this restriction is the frame of black protest. It is clear that the speaker's conception of his mission and the materials available for the accomplishment of that mission have a temporal and spatial orientation. In some sense, the black protest speaker's manifestation of this distinctiveness is dependent upon the choice or creation of audiences. This takes into account the fact that some audiences are found and others are created. When a black protest speaker addresses white audiences, the speaker is restricted by the audiences' sophistication (e.g., what they know about black language), personal attributes, and the aims of the speech. This has nothing to do with the unavailability of words; they are available in theory but may be unknown to the speaker (not part of his personal knowledge), or, if known, incompatible with the aims of the speech and, for all functional reasons, off limits. Thus, the effect is the same, and the speaker remains confined to a limited context.

It should be emphasized that the choice of protest limits the number of usable words, arguments, and strategies. Many aspects of this contextual limitation are related only to white audiences; others are more generally true and observable. The protest speaker must make sure that all the "entrances" and "exits" are covered as he speaks to white audiences; there can be no reckless abandon in language or behavior that will allow misinterpretations or misunderstandings. The protest speaker holds his cards close to the flesh when faced with white audiences.

Pirsig's comment, that the "traditional scientific method can't tell you where you ought to go, unless where you ought to go is a continuation of where you were going in the past," [38] is further complicated by the "rational" order of the established system that stands in the way of creativity and innovation. The black speaker seeks to create, to imagine a new world, to appeal to a new order, to break with the past. In fact, it is not so much the change of logic that is sought as the change of the established system. The traditional uses of language are invalidated by the insistent voices of the powerless who seek to *seize* the floor, to *take* a position, to *hold* forth in the arena of persuasion. Yet in all of this the African American speaker appeals to his or her audiences only on the basis of language that is accessible for the appropriate arguments.

Fanon knew that one could assume that the oppressed would resort to the language of the oppressor for his liberation, yet he called for a new person with a different rhetoric. Always, the protester must use different symbols, myths, and sounds than the established order. Otherwise, to speak the same language means that you will always be at a disadvantage, because the oppressed can never use the language of the established order with as much skill as the establishment. The oppressed must gain attention and control by introducing another language, another sound. Fanon's advice to the colonized, in *The Wretched of the Earth*, is to "leave this Europe where they are never done talking of Man, yet murder them everywhere they find them."[39] In this way, the black protester equalizes the power situation between himself and the oppressor, even if it is only in the area of symbolic grounding. Beyond this, of course, is the fact that such an action places the oppressed on the path to Afrocentricity; it is a liberating act, the intellectual equivalent of a slave's wave of good-bye to his master from the North side of the Ohio River.

To speak the same language as the oppressor does not lead to a positive result. To introduce new ground is the method to achieve the extreme dimensions of the protest medium. In other words, one does not assume that the protester has available the words of the established order. This is not to say that the protester's language may not *seem* to have the character of the established order. If we look at the discourse of Martin Luther King Jr., we see that his Judeo-Christian rhetoric was often put in the language of the black community. Thus, while the themes of justice, equality, and love were universal, the speaker often used logic, myth, and expressions that were derived from the culture of the oppressed. This rhetoric, in its uniqueness, attracted attention.

This behavior on the part of the black speaker has helped to shape the myth of the inaccessibility of black communication to outsiders. The form of our communication, emerging from the confrontation of slaveowner and slave, from master and property, was never open. Suspicion, distrust, and conspiracy accompanied the interactions of Africans and Europeans from the earliest periods in American history. The African who wanted to break out of the cultural and economic bondage of the American society often found even more reasons to remain suspicious of whites. Victims of a social reality that made the combination of freedom and speech dangerous for the black protest speakers, the speakers frequently resorted to modifying their speeches when talking to white audiences. Theme is seldom changed; tone and lyricism are modified. The belief exists that white audiences will not know what you mean when you refer to "Shine," "bloods on the block," "Mr. Hawkins," "simple," "when the word is given," and other "in-house" expressions; but white audiences increasingly share in the symbols of the black community, thus making more imperative an Afrocentric posture towards analysis if we want to create a context for intercultural understanding.

To this point, our discussion accounts for the situational limitations imposed on black protesters, but the Afrocentric approach identifies ways in which the black protester resists discourse limitations and creates new rhetorical ground.

If we accept the fact that the number of words in the American language is limited, we can see that, within such a system, the black protest speaker uses only a portion of the word resources available to all; he coins expressions, appeals to his environment for others, and creates combinations as he moves back and forth across code boundaries. His rhetorical actions are determined by situations both within and beyond his control. In some situations he can do something about them; in others he is helpless, unless he chooses to utilize guerrilla rhetoric.

That which the speaker expresses by the extreme dimensions of his media of words, tones, fables, myths, legends, and sounds is a sort of word subtlety, intended to subvert the established order by guerrilla rhetoric tactics.

The protest speaker's sensitivity to powerlessness in the society frees him or her to utilize the improvisational mechanisms of African American culture in responding to unpleasant situations. In some respects, H. Rap Brown, Eldridge Cleaver, Stokely Carmichael, and Bobby Seale were "jazz artists" in the 1960s. They often chose not to employ the *prevailing behavior* of white culture in their verbal responses. The police were "pigs" to Bobby Seale, and Hubert Humphrey was a "buffoon" to Eldridge Cleaver. In reply to the charge that the

Black Panthers used too much profanity, the votarists would often argue that the society was profane, poverty was profane, the government was profane, and the American system was the biggest profanity.

Confronted by a hostile legal system, which emanated from the prevailing behaviors of white American culture, the black protesters of the 1960s were frequently at odds with the system. What constituted jurisprudence and law to the white society was seen as arbitrary and violent by the protesters. Indeed, John Illo has written that "jurisprudence is the prudent justification of an absurd society of institutionalized inequity and internal contradiction. Law, and juridical logic, and grammar conspire to frustrate the original idea of a just and good society, in which all men may freely become the best that they may be." [40] The black protester, set upon the road to disalienation, seeks to return us to reformist, perhaps revolutionary, ideas.

Those fundamental ideas of liberty, fraternity, and equality—long obscured by imposed categories—are restored in the functional rhetoric of the black protester. The characteristic tonal quality of the black speaker, referred to as a lyricism by Henry Mitchell, is more often used in settings that are peculiarly black American, not white American. [41] What is at work in these situations is the sermonic style of the preacher, the archetype of the protest genre. To the extent that Jesse Jackson used this tone in his campaign for the Democratic nomination for President in 1984, he was perceived by many whites as being "too black" and not a candidate for all of the people.

There is an overwhelming opposition to the black cultural style of speech by white audiences, who see politicians more as technicians and less as moral persuaders. Certainly, Martin Luther King's "Been to the Mountaintop" speech in a Memphis church could not have been like his intellectual discourse to the Harvard University Law School; the speeches were different in tone because the speaker invented them differently. Intonation and tonal styling are substantive parts of the black speaker's invention. Furthermore, to the extent the black protest speaker employs these characteristic linguistic behaviors, he is comfortable with his audience. This is not to say that he cannot be at ease with "straight lectures" before white audiences, but that he is more likely to use nuances and idiosyncrasies that are mutually "comfortable" only with black audiences.

Therefore, the protest speaker, trying to persuade white audiences of the need for a social transformation, is simultaneously exhibiting a distrust of whites by refusing them access into the inner linguistic secrets. Even in the most intense debate over social change, the black protest speaker does not share all of his characteristic tonal patterns with white audiences; in fact, his speech further suggests what is, of course, true: Blacks and whites have different patterns of experiences. Black protest, then, is framed by characteristic rhetorical and linguistic practices that are products of a special experience, environment, and heritage.

An Organic Continuity of Protest

Among the more universal manifestations of the idea that black protest speakers consult unique contexts are the arguments invented to assault segregation, discrimination, and injustice in American society. What blacks argued a hundred years ago is still argued today. In 1843, Henry Highland Garnet noticed that "the gross inconsistency of a people holding slaves, who had themselves 'ferried o'er the wave' for freedom's sake, was too apparent to be entirely overlooked."[42]

Frederick Douglass emphasized the same theme in his famous Fourth of July speech in 1852:

> I say it with a sad sense of the disparity between us. I am not included within the pale of this glorious anniversary! Your high independence only reveals the immeasurable distance between us. The blessings in which you this day rejoice, are not enjoyed in common. The rich inheritance of justice, liberty, prosperity, and independence, be-

queathed by your fathers, is shared by you, not me. The
sunlight that brought life and healing to you, has brought
stripes and death to me. This Fourth of July is yours, not
mine. You may rejoice, I must mourn.[43]

Douglass goes on to make his point emphatically, by high-
lighting the hypocrisy of the occasion. "Whether we turn
to the declarations of the past, or to the professions of the
present, the conduct of the nation seems equally hideous and
revolting. America is false to the past, false to the present, and
solemnly binds herself to be false to the future."[44] Such language is not foreign to contemporary arguments. In the 1960s,
Malcolm X said there was no democracy, only hypocrisy.

While there may have been a proprioceptive change, as one
aspect of the problem activated a new discussion, the intent
and structure have remained constant. Attempts to provide
rhetorical solutions to political problems have produced many
duplications from one era to the next, and the operating space
seems more confining than ever.

The black protest speaker can define only two fundamental
alternatives, *integration* or *separation*, and every argument is
ultimately made for one or the other of these ends. When a
speaker has only two alternatives, speeches tend to exhibit
pat formulas. The better speakers have imaginatively organized and structured speeches from the available materials
with an end towards either integration or separation.

In relation to the two historically political goals of black
protest, one can suggest that the politics has alternated between *provincial* and *mass phenomenon*, the tactics of protest
from *verbal* to *activist*, and the ideology from *religious* to
political. The speaker decides his direction, and that choice determines the restrictions upon his invention. A protest speaker
is not always free to choose, but if he chooses the provincial
phenomenon, then certain limitations occur. For instance, if
he chooses provincial over mass political phenomena as a
channel for his aims, the instruments of mass dissemination
are not essential to the rhetorical effort. In addition, there are

technical limitations on the speaker because of his choice. In a mass situation, he would need to make some general appeals in order to save the movement from collapsing because of a too narrow focus. On a specific neighborhood problem, the speaker could concentrate on some narrow goals and make particular appeals.

Furthermore, the black speaker chooses between governing principles, for example, whether the protest will ultimately rest on religious or political bases. After a position is chosen, arguments are created or discovered that are compatible with one's rhetorical purpose. In the 1960s, H. Rap Brown could never use the language of Martin Luther King, or vice versa, yet each could use similar rhetorical strategies against segregation and discrimination. Their specific differences were inherent in their choices of governing principles, not in the nature of the problem.

All rhetorics have their strict syntax of language, with rules and laws consistent with the speaker's objectives, traditions, and abilities. This is not merely the case between H. Rap Brown or Martin Luther King Jr., Malcolm X or Jesse Jackson, Louis Farrakhan or Andrew Young, but also for the less famous orators of the street masses and the speakers in the campus rallies. The choice of syntax for discourse reflects the inviolable rules of the particular speaker's type of rhetoric. In deciding upon a governing principle, the speaker stands on the side of a certain social syntax. Houston Baker, writing of Richard Wright's understanding of the American problem, says "Wright knew that in any black life, in any white-dominated society, a life crisis of black identity—an event equivalent to such other life crises as birth, social puberty, and death—was an inevitable event." [45] Wright knew, of course, what Du Bois had said, in *The Souls of Black Folks*, about the condition of being black in a white America. Du Bois put it succinctly when he wrote in *The Souls of Black Folks* that patience would show the reader "the strange meaning of being black here at the dawning of the Twentieth Century. This meaning is not without interest to you, Gentle Reader; for the problem of the Twentieth Century is the problem of the colorline."[46]

Even in 1903 DuBois could sense a "peculiar sensation" that he called "double-consciousness" where the African looked at himself through someone else's eyes. In this respect, Wright and Du Bois carried forth the theme of a recurring response to white domination.

Addressing both the response and the condition has produced outstanding oratorical genius; the speakers and writers have had to keep the faith and yet save the day. James Cone's position is that the African American used the spirituals and the blues to speak to the same crisis of identity to which the public speeches appealed. Since the whites who practiced slavery contradicted God, blacks affirmed their "somebodiness" in attacking the whites' Godlessness. In James Cone's words, "The mountains may be high and the valleys low, but 'my Lord spoke' and 'out of his mouth came fire and smoke.'"[47] There has always been a feeling that deliverance was right around the corner; indeed, the rhetorics and lyrics of the best orators and musicians remain full of this vision.

In addition to this vision, however, was the continuing presence of the idea of blackness itself within the framework of black protest. Even the productive discourse that rose from the urban streets and the rural roads of the 1960s found some of its source in the emotional idea of black solidarity. In doing this, the protest writers and speakers were calling upon the older traditions found in Nat Turner, Henry Highland Garnet, and even W. E. B. Du Bois. It should be noted that Du Bois never intended his ideas to lead to what Marcus Garvey saw as Black Nationalism.[48]

Nevertheless, the framing of black protest can only be adequately examined by considering the peculiar experiences, creative and material, of African Americans. Certainly Du Bois' race idea is one of those emotional and cultural experiences that has been used as a motive force.

Anthony Appiah has correctly challenged Du Bois' conception of race. However, in his attempt to lay bare the kernel of truth in Du Bois' universe of discourse about race, he has crushed it unintentionally. In his critique, Appiah argues righteously that

> To put it more simply: sharing a common group history cannot be a criterion for being members of the same group, for we would have to be able to identify the group in order to identify *its* history. Someone in the fourteenth century could share a common history with me through our membership in a historically extended race only if something accounts both for his or her membership in the race of the fourteenth century and for mine in the twentieth. That something cannot, on pain of circularity, be the history of the race. Whatever holds Du Bois' races together conceptually cannot be a common history; it is only because they are bound together that members of a race at different times can share a history at all. If this is true, Du Bois' reference to a common history cannot be doing any work in his individuation of races. And once we have stripped away the sociohistorical elements from Du Bois' definition of race, we are left with the true criterion.[49]

This criterion Appiah sees as "common descent and the common impulses and strivings."[50] Of course, the real issue is not race in any scientific or quasi-scientific sense, nor even in Du Bois' socio-historical sense. What Du Bois intended, when one examines the perspective of his work, was a statement about culture, not about race. His reading of race into the picture is perhaps due in large part to the Germanic influences upon his education and the whole European enterprise of race.

Henry Louis Gates Jr. establishes the presence of race as a notion in the minds of Europe's most important thinkers. Gates claims that Hume, Kant, and Hegel made race a factor in their discussions of history, intelligence, and reason.[51] Kant goes so far as to correlate being black with being stupid! Gates responds: "Without writing, no *repeatable* sign of the workings of reason, of mind, could exist. Without memory or mind, no history could exist. Without history, no humanity, as defined consistently from Vico to Hegel, could exist."[52]

Resistance to this profoundly racist discourse prompted Africans in America to respond with their own discourses. Gates corrrectly argues that "political and philosophical discourse were the predominant forms of writing." The reason for this state of affairs was simple. The African's intellectual ability was universally denied by Eurocentric writings, and since Europeans held the monopoly of information from the sixteenth to the nineteenth century, the only action of the oppressed was reaction. In this respect, the African often found himself cast upon the moving tides of a turbulent Eurocentric ocean. Yet, as Gates says,

> The recording of an authentic black voice—a voice of deliverance from the deafening discursive silence which an enlightened Europe cited to prove the absence of the African's humanity—was the millennial instrument of transformation through which the African would become the European, the slave become the ex-slave, brute animal become the human being. So central was this idea to the birth of the black literary tradition in the eighteenth century that five of the earliest slave narratives draw upon the figure of the voice in the text—of the talking book—as crucial "scenes of instruction" in the development of the slave on the road to freedom.[53]

Resistance pours forth from the autobiographical pens of Ottabah Cugoano and Olaudah Equiano, although their political observations may have lacked candor, given their circumstances. The fact that they spoke, that they had a voice to accompany the many faces of Africans, was in itself an achievement of courage and genius.

I mention resistance in the autobiographical genre mainly because Appiah has used Du Bois' *Dusk of Dawn* as one of the sources for his analysis of Du Bois' concept of race. In the final analysis, what Appiah renders clear is Du Bois' ambivalence about race in its elusive and unfounded biological sense. What I read in Du Bois' *Dusk of Dawn* should not be "distressing" for Appiah, inasmuch as the idea of culture was taken as seriously by Du Bois as we take it today. A close reading of *The Souls of Black Folks* further supports Du Bois' culture idea.[54] Race is essentially a political concept in racist societies, but it serves no practical biological purpose for the scientist. On the other hand, the idea of culture is both significant within the structure of a resisting ideology and advantageous when we examine the causes of human misunderstanding. I must quickly add that the economic idea is, of course, a central creation of the interplay of cultural and environmental factors and therefore contributes also to our way of viewing reality.

This is no *apologia* for Du Bois' use of the term *race* in *Dusk of Dawn;* rather, it expounds his attempt at resistance in the language of his contemporaries. Du Bois, of course, was not an Afrocentricist; he was, preeminently, a Eurocentricist.[55] And since it is possible to resist within the context of a Eurocentric philosophy, though not effectively, Du Bois was a superior combatant in that arena. Using the weapons and the armor of his enemies, he achieved prominence in the quality of his struggle. Harvard and Berlin had trapped him not only in the ideology of race but in the total European outlook towards the world.

Therefore, Du Bois' rather Germanic concept of race as a unit of cultural advancement in world-historical development shows the influence of his Berlin education. Such an idea, as propagated by the German philosophers of race, is contrary to the view that culture, rather than race as a biological idea, shapes human advancement. Since race is an ambiguous term anyway, though understandably a central concept in Du Bois' training, scholarship must find some other way to speak of the motive force of a people's history.

Three ideas have been advanced to deal with the questions of blackness as a philosophical issue rather than a biological one. They are the concepts of *negritude, authenticity,* and *Afrocentricity.* None of them represents a strictly biological position, but all are centered in the socio-cultural reality of a geographical region, namely, Africa. *Negritude* is the very movement of the literary and artistic sensibilities of African intellectuals in the field of creative motifs and ethos. The originators set free the interpretative and inventive spirit that existed in African arts. Their aim was the expression of blackness as image in the world of literature and art; thus, the major practitioners were poets and writers. *Authenticity* finds its triumph in allowing people to realize themselves through their own history. Therefore, the man whose biological father was Obenga but who now calls himself Merleau, due to the interjection of an artificial history, must reclaim his historical name and, hopefully, in this process reclaim even himself. *Afrocentricity* is the most complete philosophical totalization of the African being-at-the-center of his or her existence. It is not merely an artistic or literary movement. Not only is it an individual or collective quest for authenticity, but it is above all the total use of method to effect psychological, political, social, cultural, and economic change. The Afrocentric idea is beyond decolonizing the mind.

Blackness is more than a biological fact; indeed, it is more than color; it functions as a commitment to a historical project that places the African person back on center and, as such, it becomes an escape to sanity. Therefore, when the Kenyan writer Ngugi Wa Thiong'o gives up writing in English to write in Gikuyu, he is on the path to Afrocentricity. He has chosen a difficult road, but ultimately all African writing must retrace the steps to home. This will be followed by other facets of life as we become truly conscious of ourselves. The writers who do not understand this stage in our history suffer from a deep Eurocentric consciousness. For them, it is important to show, as Du Bois could not, that the crisis of the black intellectual, as formulated later and projected by Cruse, is essentially a cultural crisis.

While Du Bois never did overthrow Eurocentric icons, he remains the major pre-Afrocentric figure in the philosophical and intellectual history of African people. Appiah writes that "though he [Du Bois] saw the dawn coming he never faced the sun."[56] However, to reverse Appiah's metaphor on the title of Du Bois' book in line with Du Bois' anticipation of Afrocentricity, I would say he saw the dusk coming as an anticipation of an Afrocentric perspective, though he could not isolate it in the fading sun of his life.

One does not have to excuse Du Bois to say that he appealed to a given universe for his resistance and, consequently, his protest; his act of rebellion, however much it was constrained, was a noble work that sought to use the available context, with all of its Eurocentric overtones, for his combat. The African American protest speaker or writer confronts the reality of the possible verbal space with every sentence of rebellion, forced, as it were, to speak a strange tongue.

Choosing Freedom

The Europeanization of human consciousness masquerades as a universal will. Even in our reach for Afrocentric possibilities in analysis and interpretation we often find ourselves having to unmask experience in order to see more clearly the transformations of our history.

Nat Turner and Henry Highland Garnet represent two powerful symbols in African American history. They stand against the tide of Europeanization in their discourse, even though the representational language of their discourse was American English. Yet the individual sense of community responsibility was in both their cases a striking motif of Afrocentricity.

In the old spiritual, "Good Lord, I done done, Good Lord, I done done, I done done what you told me to do," are all the complexities of the messianic idiom in the history of black discourse. As Shango, Anokye, Sundiata, and Tarharka receded into the past, Africans, enslaved in America, found in certain Judeo-Christian tenets the heroics of Moses, the mission of Jesus, and the heady wine of rebellion.[57] Garnet gathered the cloak to himself, but he was not the first or the last to try the delicate messianic maneuver.

The messianic idiom is the most prevalent motif in radical black discourse. In fact, in traditional black politics, such as Jesse Jackson's case, one sees its continuation. Such a formula, all-encompassing in its focus, is nothing more than the transformation of the idea of mission into a radical individualistic posture. The messiah is mission-oriented and feels a moral or supra-rational need to stand as the deliverer of the people. Our tenure in the United States is replete with acts of individual courage and valor where the *one* attempts to make a sacrifice for the *whole*. Few of these acts ever resulted in major victories, but their frequent happening is fact enough to demonstrate the internal thrust for group and even, in some cases, national salvation. To have a mission in the sense of messianism implies deliverance as an objective. No other historical motif is so present in radical black discourse, probably because so much of it is clothed in religious symbolism.

Yet messianism has no tradition in Africa; it became for the African in America, enslaved and abused, the one tenet of an apocalyptic-Judaic-Platonic heritage that immediately made sense. Domination by whites assured the individual transformations that would give meaning to the dynamics of liberation discourse even if they dressed up and went to church. The enormous emancipatory possibilities were present because someone dared to risk life to make them so. In this sense, the position I have staked out recognizes the inherent problems of a Eurocentric perspective when one treats the question of black protest discourse. Inasmuch as the protest discourse is engaged in a liberation project from extreme Eurocentric practice, it becomes impossible for a Eurocentric critique to reveal the many intricacies of the protest discourse. The reason for this is that the discourse pits itself against the universe of the critiquing ideology.

Radical spokespersons have indicated their sense of mission in the dynamism of their rhetorical style; their force of speech has given substance to the search for *something better*.

It is in the saying of *something better* that the origin of mission is indicated. *Something better* is descriptive and comparative. Social, cultural, and economic conditions have been so oppressive that we would have instilled messianism into leaders if those leaders had not possessed it. The process is mutually generative. In one sense, the people needed a leader who would be their Moses and in another sense many leaders, seeing the predicament of the people, assumed the messianic role. Assumption of such a role imposed high rhetorical taxes on the spokesperson who had to cloak himself or herself in the paraphernalia of messianism. Speeches had to possess the special *nommo* force and power that could only be delivered with a personal sense of messianism. The speaker had to believe in a special calling, not in the mere sense of a religious person who believes she or he is called to preach, but more in the classic messianic sense of believing that she or he is called to lead people out of physical bondage. This is the ingredient that separated the messianic Henry McNeal Turner from the dynamic John Jaspers. One was an activist minister and the other was an outstanding orator. Both used the social contexts of the black masses as their fountains of energy.

While messianism is not always associated with speakers, it is sometimes found in individual acts of violence where an actor believes he is doing something for the benefit of the group. Historically, the need to deliver the people from oppressive conditions motivated many rebels to rise against the slave system. Usually these rebellions involved the deaths of only one or two whites, but the slave, who was sure to die, could not control his urge to slay the oppressors and, by so doing—if only for a short while—become a deliverer, achieve liberation.

Nat Turner's Messianism

Nat Turner was the epitome of the messiah, possessing in both his person and rhetoric a clear conception of his mission. As he indicates in the *Confessions*, he is the embodiment of God's *justice and, in a sense, vengeance,* sent to punish the wayward and to warn the sinful.[58] In this belief, as expressed to Thomas Gray, who had been appointed Turner's attorney, he exemplified the complexities of the messianic idiom. When he led a group of fellow blacks in a rebellion that killed sixty whites in the Southhampton region of Virginia in 1831, he believed that he was participating in and actually materializing the will of God to cleanse the earth of sin and devils. In the 1950s and 1960s, Elijah Muhammad used similar references to whites and their treatment of African Americans. Turner put his vision in Christian terms, Muhammad chose Islamic terms; yet they both became, by virtue of their wills, the ideological *okyeames* who exhibited special knowledge.

Captured by a keen messianism that served as the most instrumental motive in the violent uprising, Nat Turner became, during his brief war against sin and evil, God's vice-regent to cleanse the earth of anti-Christ. In his mind, it was clear that this was to be a classic battle in the Christian sense—right against wrong, good against evil—whether he won or lost. Because of his reliance upon the book of *Revelation,* it is important to see the primary theme of that book. Conflict dominates the narrative, culminating in the ultimate conflict between good and evil. The struggle is not nonviolent, but carried out through war and revenge. The urgency of its message is extremely critical, making instant identification with any period in human history, but also with a special significance for slaves under the rule of slaveowners. "Fear God, and give glory to him; for the hour of his judgment is come" may have been the urgent language that moved Turner and caused him to work out the drama of death.[59] *Revelation* is a spectacular book. The actors are varied: angels; spirits; the Lamb, symbolizing Christ; the beast and Babylon, symbolizing Satan and evil. Treading the boards at center stage in the conflict, Turner saw himself as a key agent in the final victory of God over Satan. Like the writers who would follow, Turner took antislavery to be the mighty work of God.

In *Confessions,* he alludes to, draws parallels with, and as-

signs his primary motivation for killing whites to the fulfillment of prophecies. He mentions that when he was three or
four years old, he *told* something to his peers that his mother,
overhearing, said "had happened before I was born." As a
prophet deriving responsibility and authority from God, as
had John on the isle of Patmos 1,800 years before, Turner pro-
claims his predestination and outlines his duty. Thus he introduces his narrative by remarking, "I must go back to the days
of my infancy and even before I was born." From indications
given by Turner in his address to Gray, it seems that, as a
child, he was not discouraged from claiming supernatural
powers. In fact, his parents and others exclaimed he would
surely be a prophet, for the "Lord has shewn him things that
had happened before his birth."[60] Textured from birth by the
right hand of God, Nat Turner was cut from the best messianic fabric.

According to Nat Turner's testimony, he was twenty-two or
so before the spirit spoke directly to him. Three times he received the message, "Seek ye the kingdom of Heaven and all
things shall be added unto you." Of course, if he could read, as
he says he could, then this statement may well have been one
that he read in the Bible at various times. There is little reason to believe that this statement was more than a part of his
regular Bible readings. On the basis of this "revelation," he
claims that he was "ordained" for some great purpose in the
hands of the Almighty. Once again in his *Confessions,* he allows
us to see the messianistic trait emerging from his character.
Knowing his mission, and believing himself to be the leader
of the mission, he began preparing his fellow slaves for the insurrection, "I now began to prepare them for my purpose, by
telling them something was about to happen that would ter-
minate in fulfilling the great promise that had been made to
me."[61] It is not too much to ask of the slaves that they believe
him. Many slaves were extremely superstitious, and Turner
came prepared with more "hard evidence" than most that he
was somehow ordained of God to carry out this task. In addition, there were always more people ready to be believers

than were prepared to be "messiahs" with the almost certain possibility of martyrdom.

During the time of the Spirit's revelation to him, Turner escaped from an overseer and hid in the woods, and likely would have made it to freedom had he not reconsidered his duty. He had to fulfill the purpose that had been laid out for him. Subsequently, he returned to the overseer, with the internal conflict for freedom and obedience raging within him. Further revelations delineating his purpopse were made known to him through an additional vision. He saw "white spirits and black spirits engaged in battle, and the sun was darkened—the thunder rolled in the Heavens, and blood flowed in the streams."[62] What Turner apparently saw on the fields of Heaven was the prelude to the ultimate conflict he would lead against the entrenched system of slavery. In their most elemental dimensions, black and white spirits probably represented humans in earthly warfare. This explanation dispenses with the one-functional concept of the words *black* and *white* in a moral context while not totally evading the question of slavery's victims and victimizers as representatives of good and evil. Conceivably, Turner's familiarity with *Revelation* may have caused him to report a close facsimile of the fifth chapter, where seven white angels poured out the wrath of God against the evils of the earth and the rivers became blood. Whether this is true or not, Turner perceived himself as God's judgment upon the whites who held blacks in servitude.

Immediately following the vision, a voice cried out, saying "Such is your luck, such you are called to see, and let it come rough or smooth, you must surely bare it." Once again the "messianic call" comes to Turner, and he cannot reject it; he reports: "I now withdrew myself as much as my situation would permit, from the intercourse of my fellow servants, for the avowed purpose of serving the Spirit more fully." Leading the life of a prophet and thinking, meditating, plotting, Nat Turner became obsessed with his mission. The language is that of a man possessed, a man completely controlled by visions and self-persuasion. During this period of withdrawal, as happened with John the Baptist in the wilderness, the spirit revealed to him the "knowledge of the elements, the revolution of the planets, the operation of tides, and changes of the seasons."[63] He became, by virtue of withdrawal, a man who serves the purposes of *nommo;* in order to perform the work of God, he had to be made perfect.

Convinced of his perfection, he could conceive no wrong nor commit any crime; therefore, the handiwork of death, which was to be manifest at his hands, was God-ordained. And like "messianic spirits" before and after him, he moved in an artificial environment, created by his own deception and maintained by that of his followers. Now more pressing than ever, the cataclysm stood in the wings, awaiting the signal from Heaven. Turner details the signs that led to his eventual revolt:

> While laboring in the field, I discovered drops of blood on the corn as though it [*sic*] were dew from heaven—and I communicated it to many, both white and black, in the neighborhood—and I then found on the leaves in the woods hieroglyphic characters, and numbers, with the forms of men in different attitudes, portrayed in blood, and representing the figures I had seen before in the heavens. And now the Holy Ghost had revealed itself to me, and made plain the miracles it had shown me—For as the blood of Christ had been shed on this earth, and had ascended to heaven for the salvation of sinners, and was now returning to earth again in the form of dew—and as the leaves on the trees bore the impression of the figures I had seen in the heavens, it was plain to me that the Saviour was about to lay down the yoke he had borne for the sins of man, and the great day of judgment was at hand.[64]

Blood like "dew from heaven," "hieroglyphics . . . portrayed in blood," and "men in different attitudes" indicate an interrelationshp between violence and, perhaps, various degrees of sinfulness. Later in the narrative, Turner says that he saw human forms in blood on trees in the forest. The terrible battle between good and evil was now being carried to earth, to be waged by Turner against sinful men. His statement that Christ was returning to earth in the form of dew seems to suggest the constancy and pervasiveness of God's will. Continuing to prepare himself for the mission, he was baptized by the Spirit.

It is noteworthy that William Styron's celebrated *The Confessions of Nat Turner* fails to engage Turner at the level of *nommo* and duty. Styron emasculates Turner, defiling the heroic "vessel of God" and creating a Sambo. Styron uses sex repression and revolutionary tendencies as the emotional and psychological fuel on which Turner runs. Perhaps Murray records Styron's problem best when he says that the author was "either unable or unwilling to bring himself to make a truly intimate and profoundly personal identification with the black protagonist whose heroism he himself has chosen to delineate and whose sense of life he has elected to impersonate, if not emulate."[65] Styron neither understood nor appreciated the powerful folk hero Turner had become. Turner did not signify defeat, but courage and audacity and this boldness came from the power of his calling.

On the 12th of May, 1828, Turner heard "a loud noise in the heavens, and the Spirit instantly appeared," saying to him that the "Serpent was loosened, and Christ had laid down the yoke he had borne for the sins of men," and that he "should take it on and fight against the Serpent for the time was fast approaching when the first should be last and the last should be first."[66] These statements, exceptionally complex, seem to mean that if in fact the day of judgment was at hand, God himself would deal out punishment for the sinners. However, it is possible that, in Turner's Afrocentric theological system, only men, as God's agents, could carry out providential decrees on earth. Therefore, when the Serpent was loosened, Turner, as God's viceroy, had to rise up and slay him, regardless of the consequences. Such was the divine mission that obsessed Nat Turner from early childhood to maturity and blossomed into the revolt he led in 1831.

Turner was an astute man with a discerning intelligence. He had learned to read and write when it was illegal for slaves to have books or for whites to teach them the alphabet. Native intelligence had early marked him as a leader of his peers. What made him believe that he could carry out the mission? Certainly the odds were against any overthrow of the organized slave system and its sympathizers. But Turner had the precedents of Revelation on his side. If God had laid Babylon to waste "in one hour," then surely he could oversee the triumph of Turner's forces. God was clearly on his side. And there was also an implied promise of support: "And all the trees of the field shall know that I the Lord have brought down the high tree, have exalted the low tree, have dried up the green tree, and have made the dry tree to flourish."[67] Furthermore, success was relative, and after all, Turner asked, "Was not Christ crucified?" In his mind, martyrdom contained the very seeds of victory; he had only to plant his message deeply.

Although the indomitable messianism moved in his mind and stirred his emotions, Turner seemed to sense the difficulty of total liberation of the slaves. The language of finality betrays his bloody heroics; and a ritualized farewell supper, like Christ's before the cleansing campaign, may well have suggested his reservations. Actually, he did not see his battle merely in the secular sense of a slave insurrection. When asked by Thomas Gray to give an account of his activities, he replied, "Sir, you have asked me to give a history of the motives which induced me to undertake the late insurrection, as you call it."[68] He continued to present his narrative in the metaphysics of a holy war.

There is a sense of outrage that a white man could dare ask why the insurrection occurred. Nat Turner was allegory, the total embodiment of meaning and substance. There was nothing in his person or his mission to betray the Afrocentric thrust for victory over slavery, triumph of the spirit, and the breaking of chains. If he had to answer this white querist, he would appeal to the metaphysical; perhaps in the alchemical realm there was some way to explain why the slaves had to revolt. Belief in his own righteousness and perfection went with him to the gallows. Regardless of what men did to his body, his spirit would reside in peace and glory with God. Even Thomas Gray had to notice, with awe, Turner "clothed with rags and covered with chains; yet daring to raise his manacled hands to heaven with a spirit soaring above the attributes of man."[69]

In careful examination of Turner's own words, one finds that his motivation had strong roots in both African and Christian theology. In his description of his childhood, the solidarity he felt with the environs, the approval and support he received from his parents, grandmother, owner, and peers engineered a solid foundation for a powerful ego and an unbreakable spirit. While the mission-oriented spokesperson, such as Marcus Garvey during his Back-to-Africa Campaign, is common, the person possessed from youth with the idea of mission is rare. His parents strengthened the belief that he had supernatural powers by saying that he "was intended for some great purpose, which they had always thought from certain marks on [his] head and breast."[70] Hence the emergence of a messianic self-concept that flowered with each announcement of support and approval and became crucial in the latter, more cognitive phase of planning. The word magic of Turner—and all magic is word magic—was the source and end of his personal power.

Nat Turner's grandmother looms in his life like one of the ancient Yoruba *iyami* (mothers). She represents a source of wisdom and guidance in the midst of uncontrollable forces, and Turner is the answer to the disharmony and discord of slavery and persecution. As the *iyami* stand to the propitiation and adoration offered in the performance of the Yoruba *gelede* dance, so does Turner's grandmother appear in his development and actions. The Yoruba have a saying about *gelede: Ojú tó wo geledé ti dópin iran* (The eyes that have seen gelede have seen the end of drama). In African American resistance discourse, Nat Turner's revolt was a ritualized offering to the female ancestors, a feast of deliverance, a dance of celebration to his African grandmothers; and she was explicitly and historically precisely African.

Of his precociousness, he stated:

> My grandmother, who was very religious, and to whom I was much attached—my master, who belonged to the church, and whom I often saw at prayers, noticing the singularity of my manners, I suppose, and my uncommon intelligence for a child, remarked I had too much sense to be raised, and if I was, I would never be of any service to anyone as a slave—To a mind like mine, restless, inquisitive and observant of everything that was passing, it is easy to suppose that religion was the subject to which my attention was now directed. The manner in which I learned to read and write, not only had great influence on my own mind, as I acquired it with the most perfect ease, so much so, that I have no recollection whatever of learning the alphabet—but to the astonishment of the family, one day when a book was shewn to me to keep me from crying, I began spelling the names of different objects—this was a source of wonder to all in the neighborhood, particularly the blacks—and this learning was constantly improved at all opportunities.[71]

Religion figures heavily in this statement and must be explored in view of the intellectual poverty of plantation life. As an important cultural component of Southern society, both black and white, religion and a neo-Greek orientation provided the primary diversion and referent point. For the slave, furthermore, the biblical lessons and stories, even in the restricted context imposed by white censors, supplied an idea of human relationships.

One of the fundamental themes of Greek civilization is that

man is a social being who achieves his highest state in political talk. Moreover, the Greeks conceived thought to be inseparable from its public expression, a precondition of which was "common sense," that is, that aspect of reality that the individual recognizes and that appears to anyone who has a similar perspective and provides the foundation of public endeavor. Nat Turner sees the essential human quality of talk and takes emotional and personal involvement to a higher level than is found in the Greek conception.

Anyway, this conception of man-as-speaker suffered from Platonic attacks on sophistry and upon Athenian public life in general, and as a consequence gave to Western thought a distinctively antirhetorical cast long after Greek Sophism itself had vanished. Plato was committed to philosophical solitude; social intercourse necessarily destroys the philosophic act. Furthermore, Plato rejected the realm of appearance; the sense world distracts and confuses the philosopher; it is only the "eye of the soul" that can intuit the transcendent, invariant realm of knowledge. This bifurcation of reality had the disastrous impact of denying the "arts of appearance" any legitimate connection to genuine thought and placed Greek thought against wholistic thought.

Augustine, an African, completed the separation of thought from sense appearance begun by Plato, further divorcing rhetoric from its intellectual roots. John Locke's attacks on innate ideas, the emphasis of the "new science" on naive sense experience, the eschewal of value and normal discourse, and the emphasis on historical consciousness are other factors responsible for the cleavage between appearance and being in Western communication. In appealing to an Afrocentric thrust into human understanding, I am challenging the irrelevant orthodoxy initially formulated in the ancient Greek distortions of the Egyptian (Kemetic) notion of rhetoric that depended upon the primacy of harmony and balance. The African concept of rhetoric, like dance, was preeminently a social act. The Bible, quite monumentally, served as Nat Turner's primer in an intellectual sense while his African orientation to social action, kept alive by his oppression, served as his guide to rebellion. All of this, mind you, was in spite of the neo-Greek referents of Southern plantation life.

In addition, the Bible gave guidelines from which inferences and judgments could be made about the immediate social milieu. The only book Turner was perhaps ever able to read in depth, because of accessibility, was the Bible, which stimulated his imagination and at every turn supported his call to mission. What Turner saw as overwhelming approval from his peer group also confirmed his ideas of mission. At the time and later, he says, "I was not addicted to stealing in my youth, nor have ever been—yet such was the confidence of the Negroes in the neighborhood, even at this early period of my life, in my superior judgment, that they would often carry me with them . . . to plan for them."[72]

What surfaces in Turner's *Confessions* as a belief in his mission to alleviate black suffering marks a black messianism that has occasionally appeared in the rhetoric of black spokesmen. Apparently, the images employed and statements made in verbal discourses betray the speakers' awareness of their people's oppression. The radical discourses of David Walker, Henry Highland Garnet, William E. B. Du Bois, Nat Turner, Marcus Garvey, and Malcolm X (El Hajj Malik Shabazz) reveal the uniformity of the messianic idiom. In mass leaders such as Frederick Douglass, Booker T. Washington, and Martin Luther King we see a similar belief in their special mission. Perhaps King in contemporary times, more than any other black spokesman, exemplified the messianic idiom with "I have been to the mountaintop." It is in the vision, the possibility, the hope in the midst of despair that the messianic notion finds its right to be. Nat Turner, epitomizing black messianism, was both person and process, and his *Confessions* remains to document the language of a man in tune with fundamental desires of Africans to be free.

Turner's messianism anticipated the ultimate call for estrangement from white America, the totalization of the feelings against racism and prejudice. Thus, even after emancipation, African Americans sought to enunciate and propagate the idea of back-to-Africa. The discourse that accompanied that movement I call the *rhetoric of psychical and physical emigration.*

Henry Highland Garnet

In the nineteenth century, no social movement captured the imaginations and commanded the minds of intellectuals, black and white, more than the antislavery effort. Numerous speeches were made by black and white abolitionists, bent on the death of slavery, and since then, rhetorical studies have been made of the significant white abolitionists;[73] however, black spokespersons for abolition seem to have been invisible, not so much because they were ineffective among their contemporaries, but more because rhetorical critics have tended to look through a glass "whitely."[74] During the entire course of antislavery agitation, nevertheless, such men as Charles Remond, Frederick Douglass, and Henry Highland Garnet were in the front ranks of the movement. Their voices, stronger than most, and their messages, keener than most, whipped and lashed an abominable system. But like the ranks of the white abolitionists, the black crusaders were badly split on the issue of means.[75] Among the African abolitionists, Henry Highland Garnet was the leader of the discordant voices; the majority wanted moral suasion, but he demanded violent insurrection. During a time when few black abolitionists envisioned the need for violence, Garnet pleaded before the 1843 convention of blacks for insurrection. Where did this revolutionary voice come from?

No black antislavery orator was by temperament and training better suited to embrace militancy than Garnet. Born a slave in New Market, Maryland in 1815, he escaped with his parents to New York at the age of nine.[76] Garnet received his basic education at a private school in New York that was operated by free blacks. As a young man of twenty, he organized a hundred and fifty youths into the Garrison Literary and Benevolent Association, a group more interested in revolution than literature. The same year, he was invited to attend an academy at Canaan, New Hampshire, but the move was aborted when certain members of Canaan's population dispelled any notion that it was the Promised Land.[77] A mob of irate residents marched onto the campus and destroyed the school building. However, Garnet was befriended by a minister, Beriah Green, who encouraged him to continue ministerial training at Oneida Institute in Whitestown, New York.[78] Although the Oneida experience served to increase his ministerial desires, it did not lessen the bitterness from the Canaan experience. Turning his natural gift for the platform to persistent agitation against slavery was an exceedingly simple task, made easier by the harshness of his childhood, his status as a fugitive slave, and his religious fervor. After graduation in 1840, Garnet held numerous ministerial posts, from Kingston, Jamaica, to New York City, simultaneously developing his speaking skills and popularizing his reputation as a fervent antislavery spokesman.[79] During the Civil War he was an active supporter of the Union, exhorting blacks to join the Union Army and strike blows for the freedom of their brothers. His eloquent speeches prompted the House of Representatives to invite him to speak in Congress, celebrating the Thirteenth Amendment to the Constitution. After his speech to Congress, he served as president of Avery College in Pittsburgh, Pennsylvania, and had a successful career as an educator. When he died, in 1882, he was serving as U.S. Minister to Liberia.

By 1843, Garnet was considered an outstanding public speaker—brilliant, articulate, certain to have a verbal key to every political house in the antislavery campaign. Of the chief black abolitionists, Garnet was the most generously endowed with a combination of intellectual discipline and rhetorical talents. An intensely emotional man, inspirational and eager, who liked to have his voice heard on significant matters, Garnet was always ready with a speech or a resolution. A militant preacher, he justified violence to his religious conscience by believing that the end, abolition, was larger than the means. An activist, he conquered his fear by remembering his slave childhood, and found the memory sufficient to neutralize cowardice. He opened the windows of his imagination to every conceivable solution for abolition of slavery, and concluded that violent revolution was both practical and essential. As a public speaker, Garnet was of the lineage of Uthman dan Fodio and Patrick Henry rather than Okomfo Anokye or John Adams. Like Fodio and Henry, he was an eloquent crier, though never quite as inconsistent, and always more troubled by the honesty of his speech than by the effect.

All his public life, Garnet's rhetorical emotionalism was constrained by his sincerity and ministerial loyalties. The pulpit was a hard taskmaster. As a child of the congregation, certain to be damned for militant behavior, his public speeches attested to great skill as he maneuvered to be true to himself and to his church. As one of the leading sons of the American church, made so by his powerful declamations against injustice and slavery, it pained him to denounce the church's hypocrisy. To repudiate the church for its duplicity and to damn the Christian religion for its conformity to slavery while remaining honest to himself was perhaps one of Garnet's greatest rhetorical accomplishments. (Archbishop Desmond Tutu and the Reverend Allan Boesak, both of South Africa, have stated their psychological pain in having to condemn the Christian church while serving it. Like Garnet before them, they are trapped by the hypocrisy of their institutions.)

Having been shaped in the disciplined mold of Presbyterianism, Garnet's religion was the very blood of his antislavery activities, and repudiation of religion would have taken the sting out of his rhetoric. The material of which he was fashioned would allow him to be dishonest neither to himself nor the church; thus Garnet's speeches are masterpieces, not of audience adaptation but of unblemished sincerity. Indeed, his impassioned rhetoric, mental acumen, and concentrated militancy made him the outstanding revolutionary of his day, although for quiet rhetorical artistry he was not worthy to untie Frederick Douglass's shoestrings.

Unlike the black preachers who grew from Baptist or Methodist soil, Garnet's mental bent was less keen to subliminal fantasies and vivid images, due to his Presbyterian training.[80]

Instead, the language of his speeches and sermons was simple and concrete, employing common figures and illustrations. But the humble trope or figure became highly exalted in his dynamic delivery.

The occasion of Henry Highland Garnet's most militant, and most famous, speech was the National Convention of Colored Citizens in Buffalo, New York, August 21–24, 1843. Seventy outstanding delegates from Northern states assembled to assess the race's progress, chart strategy, and appeal for total black unity. In attendance among the delegates were such notable orators as Charles Lenox Remond, Frederick Douglass, and William Wells Brown, each with his special sensibility. Undaunted by this august array of eloquent campaigners, the twenty-eight-year-old Garnet gave his "Address to the Slaves of the United States of America" to a startled audience.[81] The speech provoked considerable debate among men whose antislavery credentials were beyond question, and when the vote was taken on the controversial address as the resolution of the group, it was rejected by one vote. The free blacks, beguiled by caution, took the moderate path of urging moral suasion rather than violent insurrection. A few years later John Brown, convinced that violence was the road to liberty, had the speech published at his own expense. Thus, despite the thin margin by which the address was rejected at the assembly in 1843, by 1848 Garnet had developed into a leading revolutionary.

What did Garnet say that sent tremors through his audience? Why did his speech set off such vehement controversy among men joined in the antislavery fight? Was he a demagogue, or a political realist? The answers to these and similar questions are best found in the speech itself, the volatile context of antislavery agitation, the influences upon the speaker, and Afrocentric considerations.

Immediately afer a terse introduction, Garnet said: "Brethren and Fellow Citizens" (which reminds one of Malcolm X's equally acid openings, except that in Garnet's day women did not attend public meetings), then charged that the delegates had been accustomed "to meet together in National Conventions, to sympathize with each other" over the conditions of the slaves.[82] Indeed, talk had proved extremely cheap since the initial meetings of the Colored Citizens, when the price of political involvement was paid with expensive actions. Garnet's indictment scored a direct hit. In 1827 the First General Assembly of Colored Citizens had met in Boston, the womb of radicalism, to seek black unity and to discuss ways to help the slaves. Meetings of one kind or another had been held annually or semiannually on the slavery issue ever since, and no one had introduced resolutions of action. Speeches proliferated like so much fallout but were certain not to have any immediate effect on the slaves' liberation. Thus Garnet's opening statement served notice that he had little sympathy with the past actions of the conventions. Speaking as to the slaves, he said, "We have been contented in sitting still and mourning over your sorrows, earnestly hoping that before this day your sacred liberties would have been restored."[83] Again, Garnet accused the antislavery giants of do-nothingness in the liberation of the slaves. In fact, the introduction threw a good deal of light on Garnet's rhetorical strategy in the remainder of the speech: he lashed the free blacks as he whipped out the emotions of the enslaved, because of the inaction of both in the face of oppression.

In developing the speech, Garnet exploited the gap between theory and practice to establish the cruelty and villainy of Christians. Inconsistency between ideal and reality, between theory and practice, has always been the classic force that gives aggressive rhetoric its energy. And in the case of Christians and slavery, the chasm was not bridgeable in the mind or rhetoric of Henry Highland Garnet. He contended that "the first dealings they [Africans] had with men calling themselves Christians exhibited to them the worst features of corrupt and sordid hearts."[84] A stout supporter of the Christian's God and loyal to the church, even at the risk of being unloyal to his brethren, Garnet saw the Christian's complicity in slavery as godless and unspeakable. The sacred documents and preachers saw one thing and the people in the pews saw another, wholly different thing. Furthermore, what *was* done was harmful to black people. Consider Garnet's disdain that "slavery had stretched its dark wings of death over the land, the church stood silently by—the priests prophesied falsely, and the people loved to have it so."[85] (Even Garnet had been influenced by Eurocentric images of the black angel of death.) Echoing his rhetorical master, David Walker, who had written in 1829 that the "Christian Americans were the most cruel people on earth,"[86] Garnet saw the church as distorting the image of Christianity. Christian Americans hypocritically blamed England for the horrible system of slavery, but once the colonies were free they added new links to the slaves' chains.

With the stage set to highlight the inexcusable apathy of his brethren, free and enslaved, and the cruel villainy of the Christians, Garnet had one more prop to put into place. He must hammer his own theology into the religious molds of his brethren. They must be convinced that his theological position was justified and in keeping with their own religious beliefs. It is on this point that Garnet demonstrated his rhetorical genius. In view of the extreme suffering of the slaves, he urged upon them two major considerations on slavery: (1) "to such degradation it is *sinful* [italics mine] in the extreme for you to make voluntary submission," and (2) "neither God nor Angels, or just men, command you to suffer for a single moment. Therefore it is your solemn and imperative duty to use every means, both moral, intellectual, and physical, that promises 'success.'"[87]

Such a strong argument for insurrection, based upon morality, was meant to overpower whatever religious objections the free and enslaved blacks might have. It is not simply wrong, but "sinful in the extreme" to submit voluntarily to slavery. A crucial moral issue has been inserted into the political and social predicament of the religiously motivated slave. Rebellion is given a moral sanction; and if not directly authorized by God, certainly not condemned by him. Furthermore, Garnet argued that slaves had a "solemn and imperative duty" to use every means, whether moral, intellectual, or physical. For the nineteenth-century slave, the word *duty* had a familiar ring to it, and Garnet wisely chose to employ it in the same context with resistance and insurrection. For the Garrisonians, such as Remond and Douglass, not yet ready for other than moral and intellectual means, this must have been an uneasy moment in Garnet's speech. But to Garnet, slavery was not merely distasteful, it was abominable, and as such demanded a drastic response: "He counsels insurrection motivated by moral commitment. Look around you, and behold the bosoms of your loving wives heaving with untold agonies! Hear the cries of your poor children! Remember the stripes your fathers bear. Think of your wretched sisters, loving virtue and purity, as they are driven into concubinage and are exposed to unbridled lusts of incarnate devils."[88]

Thus the slaves must tell their owners, plainly, that they are "determined to be free." As words alone may evoke no reaction, or an adverse reaction, from the slaveowners, Garnet proposed a contingency plan. "You had far better all die—die immediately, than live as slaves, and entail your wretchedness upon your posterity."[89] At this point in the speech, heroic examples trod upon each other's heels as Garnet praised Denmark Veazy, Nathaniel Turner, Joseph Cinque, and Madison Washington. In passing, he invoked the names of Moses, Hampden, Tell, Bruce, Wallace, L'Ouverture, Lafayette, and George Washington. Appealing to pride as well as shame, Garnet urged the slaves to follow the path of "those who have fallen in freedom's conflict."[90]

Although the tone of the discourse had been established early, it was the peroration that marked Garnet as a militant advocate, bent on insurrection. Witness the call to arms: "Brethren, arise, arise! Strike for your lives and liberties, now is the day and the hour. Let every slave throughout the land do this, and the days of slavery are numbered. You cannot be more oppressed than you have been—you cannot suffer greater cruelties than you [suffer] already. Rather die freemen than live to be slaves. Remember that you are four millions." Furthermore, he concluded, "Let your motto be resistance! Resistance! Resistance!"[91]

Such was the language of Henry Highland Garnet before the star-studded audience at Buffalo. However, while the arguments were clear and sharp *vis-à-vis* the slaves' obligations, nothing was required of the free blacks. If Garnet's message could have been disseminated to four million slaves (most of whom could not read), they might have been persuaded to participate in an insurrection. Had Garnet counselled the free black to infiltrate the South in efforts to organize the slaves, his plan may have appeared more practicable. But even that kind of plan for insurrection would not have moved the Garrisonians.

When Garnet finished speaking, a vigorous debate ensued that divided the conference into two philosophical camps. The Garrisonians were not about to relinquish antislavery leadership to militants who they feared would disrupt the cooperation between blacks and whites in the abolition movement. When the din of the debate ended and a single voice called for the question, the resolution failed—as had the sentiments of the delegates—by one vote. The vote, like the polarization during the debates, reflected a fundamental cleavage in the black antislavery movement. Rejecting Garnet's resolution, by even so slight a margin, the delegates had voted to remain unprovocative.

Their decision had all the features of capitulation to a Eurocentric view of the struggle for black liberty. Fear of offending white political and social interests grasped the minds of the delegates in a political vise, tightened by the overwhelming cultural and image context of white Americans. They acted against Garnet to demonstrate their solidarity with their white allies.

Beyond the immediate reaction to Garnet's rhetoric is the fact that his style introduced emotion into the deliberative arena. There could be no escape from Garnet's improvisation on the theme of slavery and its cruelty. He felt it deeply and spoke of it as one committed to solidarity with the slaves. There could be no answer to the horrible bondage of the slaves but resistance and struggle. Therefore the vote against Garnet's position was probably as much a reaction against his style as his substance. The acceptance of the traditions of white deliberative bodies obviously meant that any expressive *nommo* was to be kept at a minimum in such circles. Militant black rhetoric of resistance and struggle, spoken with emotion, has always caused uneasiness in the United States. There is, even among Africans at times, the attempt to keep the lid on the explosive discourse that lurks just below the surface of any public discussion of human rights.

Five years later, Garnet produced a volume that contained David Walker's *Appeal to the Colored Citizens of the World* and his *Address to the Slaves of the United States.*[92] In 1849, the Ohio State Convention of Colored Citizens authorized the purchase and distribution of five hundred copies of the work.[93] Thus the circulation of Garnet's racial ideas continued, despite his rebuff by the National Convention of Colored Citizens in 1843.

Garnet's speech had helped to establish the tradition of the mission of liberation; it set out the obstacles and the actions; it created the tensions that always accompany the messianic idiom. Just as some people before Garnet, others after him took the baton and declared the urgency of deliverance. He had demonstrated, with one speech, a whole universe of discourse, as had been the case with Nat Turner's insurrection and subsequent "confessions." The migration of ideas to the fertile ground of the twentieth century meant that an Afrocentric response to African American realities would come closer to perfection in the movement of back-to-Africa rhetoric.

Africa as Concept

The Back-to-Africa Movement in the early twentieth century was a concrete manifestation of the discourse of frustration; it was African Americans' radical critique of the American Dream. As a movement with mass appeal among working-class blacks, the Back-to-Africa Campaign represents the first major collective response to racism and the American condition, the antislavery campaigns notwithstanding. Directly or indirectly, nearly ten million lives were touched by the movement over a period of ten years.

The language, scope, and arguments of the Back-to-Africa Movement were tantamount to crusades for freedom and sanity, underscoring the African's essential search for dignity and cultural renewal in a strange land. Those who preached the rhetoric of return were fundamentally celebrating the survival of an African sensibility in the African American. Some Western communicationists have been too caught up with the concept of rhetoric as a transaction in the marketplace between people of similar perspectives. Afrocentric interpretation introduces a new, critical perspective into the nature of human discourse, especially when that discourse emerges from the cutting edges of rejection and resistance.

Back-to-Africa

Back-to-Africa expresses, as a movement, a unique relationship to society because it ensures a degree of power. In this movement, dialogue with the external society is only sought when such relationship is absolutely necessary. Those times are few, but they do come. The central task seems to be enlisting blacks into the Back-to-Africa Campaign, which means that persuasion becomes a primary function of the person who speaks as the situation demands. Back-to-Africa speakers are motivated by social and political configurations that sanction them. And to view Back-to-Africa as leader-centered or message-centered is to see only one part of the social movement. (I will discuss shortly the various roles of leaders and messages.) The fundamental critical thrust of the movement must be aimed at its peculiar position *vis-à-vis* the total society.

Back-to-Africa, the classic example of a movement of those who have lost (or never had) political or social faith in America, exists in opposition to the external society, but unlike most social movements in America, its aim is withdrawal. As such, it has occupied a significant position in black political thought.

Two basic objectives have tended to dominate the endless discussion of black liberation. Both begin at the same conditional reality and seek the same ultimate goal. While these objectives, integration and separation, have often operated concurrently, each with its own constituency, one or the other tends to take center stage in a given epoch. We may view them as *alternatives*, the principal choices isolated by blacks in search of an answer to the race riddle in America.

What I have chosen to call *rhetorical manifestations* are the principal themes enunciated by the various spokespersons as they move towards one or the other alternative. Rhetorical manifestations answer the question, How have blacks dealt thematically with the goals of integration and separation? In an analysis, one would also want to examine the spokesman's use of other rhetorical measures in connection with this thematic expression. Investigation of the rhetoric of Booker T. Washington, W. E. B. Du Bois, Marcus Garvey, and Elijah Muhammad shows that these men were exercised by the themes relevant to their choice of *alternatives*. Persistently overshadowed by the themes designed to bring about integration, the Back-to-Africa Movement, at one time the largest mass movement in American society, has always been at the core of black thought.

The Return Myth

Near the turn of the century a black sharecropper, writing to the American Colonization Society, exclaimed, after telling of the horrors perpetrated on blacks, "Oh may God help us to get out from here to Africa."[94] Later, Marcus Garvey underscored the problem:

> It can plainly be seen, that in the question of self preservation and self interest the whites nowhere, whether in America, England or France, are going to give way to the

Negro to the detriment of their own. We need not look for
constitutional protection, or even for philanthropic Christian sympathy, because if that is to be shown it will be to
the race that is able to bestow it. Hence the UNIA [Uni-
versal Negro Improvement Association] has but one solution for this great problem, and that is to work unceas-
ingly for the bringing about of a National Homeland for
Negroes in Africa."[95]

Garvey, while not the first, but certainly the greatest Back-
to-Africa *spokesman*, urged withdrawal as a form of action:
"Some of our leaders in the Negro race flatter themselves into
believing that the problem of black and white in America will
work itself out, and that all the Negro has to do is to be humble,
submissive and obedient and everything will work out well in
the 'sweet bye and bye.'"[96] And Bishop Henry Turner argued: "I
would make Africa a place of refuge, because I see no other
shelter from the stormy blast, from the red tide of persecution,
from the horrors of American prejudice."[97]

Men like Garvey and Turner capitalized on the strong belief, created by the harsh realities of being black in white
America, that there could never be harmonious relations
among blacks and whites. That Garvey, and Turner before
him, could attract hundreds of thousands of blacks with the
rhetoric of emigrationism can only be understood in the light
of what must be called the ultimate political realization. Such
people have come to believe, and to argue, that blacks can
only find happiness in Africa; and they have begun to believe
that integration is, at worst, impossible, and at best, imprac-
ticable. Thus those who have listened intently to the rhetoric
of Garvey, Turner, or Aaron Henry (of the contemporary Republic of New Africa) have come to see new possibilities. When
men have gloried in the University of Sankore, felt pride and
awe at the mention of Zimbabwe, and ceased to dread the
rain forests, they have become exceptional missionaries, convincing others that Africa is the place for the African.

The leaders of Back-to-Africa expressed their dreams in

their deeds. Often driven by a sense of mission, they have become vulnerable because of the incompatible demands of their ultimate objectives and the necessities of the present moment. This phenomenon is not unique to the Back-to-Africa movement but is a pervasive aspect of any movement that relies so heavily upon the concept of the spoken word in the public presentation of the movement's position.[98] Thus when finances are in shambles, competing imperatives of time and theme are impinging upon the organization, and ships fail to appear that would take the faithful to the Promised Land; the halo of mission seems dull. Talk becomes empty, people complain of bombastic rhetoric, and votarists seek elsewhere to be filled.

The leaders of Back-to-Africa movements have always assumed a central role in directing "the people" out of bondage. Despite the paucity of information regarding the African continent in the nineteenth century, the votarists of Back-to-Africa found remarkable interest and enthusiasm, due in part to the physical and psychological terror inflicted on the black population. Eloquent speakers, with rich imaginations and forceful deliveries, aroused in the downtrodden, the wretched, the image of a Chosen Land.

Since the relationship between religion and social progress was often symbiotic in early African American movements, it is not surprising that this remained the case into the twentieth century with the major proponents of Back-to-Africa.

The most prominent and outspoken Back-to-Africa advocate between the Civil War and the First World War was Bishop Turner. Turner possessed "a dominating personality, a biting tongue, and a pungent vocabulary which gained him high office and wide audiences, first in Georgia Reconstruction Politics and later in the African Methodist Episcopal Church."[99] It was as a travelling evangelist for the white Southern Methodist Church that he discovered the pervasiveness of prejudice in American society, even within the church. In New Orleans in 1858, his nascent black nationalism found something refreshing: a church operated and controlled by blacks, the A.M.E. He immediately joined it and became one of the leading preachers, pastoring first in Baltimore and then in Washington. "After the general emancipation he became openly belligerent and urged the newly freed slaves to defend themselves vigorously when attacked or insulted." [100] Even as a freeborn person, he had experienced enough racism and had seen enough cruelty to agitate for strong black organizations to combat prejudice. Devoting much of his energy to establishing the A.M.E. in Georgia, he argued that only in a church governed solely by blacks could the recently freed black find freedom to express himself. [101]

When the national Republican Party was trying to organize the people in Georgia, Turner, because he was well-known among party leaders, was their choice to organize the freedmen. After he called the first Republican state convention in Georgia, he was elected to the 1867 Georgia Constitutional Convention and in 1868 was elected to the state legislature. No sooner was he elected and the legislature convened than his highest hope was dashed, when his white colleagues tried to disqualify blacks from holding elective office. On the House floor, Turner gave a vehement speech denouncing the attempts of the House to dismiss the black representatives and demanding his rights as a free citizen. Turning to the blacks in the House, he said, "White men are not to be trusted; they will betray you. . . . Black men, hold up your heads. . . . This thing means revolution." [102]

The dismissal of the blacks made Turner's latent nationalism surface; he talked up black power in the state and encouraged blacks to vote the whites out of power. He applied for the office of U.S. Minister to Haiti, but was given the job of postmaster in Macon, Georgia. As the first black postmaster in the state, he became a rallying point for the masses, looking for some assurance that blacks could "make it" in America. But two weeks after he was made postmaster, the local whites succeeded in getting him dismissed, claiming theft and fraud. Disappointed, frustrated, without an effective political power base, he returned to his church and started his campaign to get blacks to leave for Africa, arguing that the United States was a white man's nation and that blacks must leave.[103]

Depression, anxiety, frustration, then, were the marks of Turner's conversion; he was a victim of the white man's nationalism, and his response was a black man's nationalism. He urged members of the A.M.E. to follow the "urge of a mysterious providence," saying, "Return to the land of your Father."[104] Taking his own advice, the bishop toured West Africa to get on-the-spot information, then returned to the United States more convinced than ever that if the black man is ever to acquire wealth or prestige, he will never do it by snubbing his native land. Turner's African trip made him much more effective as a nationalistic preacher and placed him in the forefront of black spokesmen in his day. When he died in 1915, he—more than any other black person—had not only directed the Back-to-Africa Movement but had also shaped its course for years to come. His relentless emigration rhetoric provided the arguments for other emissaries of the movement, and gave Marcus Garvey a ready-made base.

Thus when Garvey came ashore in America in 1916, he found a profound disillusionment among blacks, stemming directly from their humiliation in American society and stirred by the earlier emigrationists, most notably, Henry Turner. With Booker T. Washington dying in the same year as Turner, the black community was left without a popular leader. As no one rose to continue Washington's work, Garvey, inspired by Washington, followed in Turner's footsteps and called for emigration to Africa. The pace of integration was frustratingly slow, discontent was exceedingly widespread, and blacks came to feel that more vigorous measures had to be taken to achieve political goals. The passions and needs of the time demanded a special brand of rhetoric to galvanize the downtrodden masses; Garvey was the rhetor.

But Garvey believed that whites would place obstacles even in the African's attempt to emigrate to Africa. Indeed, much of black protest thought—like the integrationist Muslims' of the

1970s in Alabama, trying to be either good capitalists or separationists—has dealt with overcoming the hurdles placed by
whites. In fact, whites not only tried to hinder or prevent the
Back-to-Africa Campaign, but also Garvey saw them occupying the homeland itself.

> The Negroes of the world say, "We are striking home-
> wards towards Africa to make her the big black republic."
> And in the making of Africa a big black republic, what is
> the barrier? The barrier is the white man; and we say to
> the white man who now dominates Africa that it is to his
> interest to clear out of Africa now, because we are coming
> not as in the time of Father Abraham, 200,000 strong, but
> we are coming 400,000,000 [strong].[105]

Such language was sooner or later to bring him into conflict with whites who saw in such rhetoric signs of danger.
In 1921 the FBI investigated UNIA's attempt to purchase a
ship, calling Garvey "a radical agitator who advocates the
overthrow of the United States Government by force and violence."[106] Furthermore, the UNIA was said to be "the communist party which is affiliated with the Russian Soviet Government."[107] His troubles soon began to eat away at the fabric of
his organization. Garvey, though no friend to the Commu-
nists, became a target for the FBI, who made him one of the
first scapegoats for the FBI's Communist hunt. Financial difficulties, combined with the growing attempt of black intellectuals to dissociate themselves from Garvey, made him more
vulnerable to attacks by government officials. And in 1927 he
was deported to Jamaica, after his sentence for mail fraud
had been commuted by President Coolidge.[108]

Turner and Garvey, more than any other black spokespersons, spoke to the restlessness of the black masses in America.
Appealing to the pride and dignity of their black listeners,
they showed the far-reaching power of black nationalism for
an oppressed people.

The Afrocentric analysis of a Back-to-Africa movement, like

investigations of other movements built and sustained by the spoken word and conscious action, must consider the spokesperson's conception of existence, history, society, and value as expressed in his language. Such consideration, treating a special perspective about society and history, and examining a bitterness towards fate (not because of blackness but because of blackness in white America), identifies the overmastering metaphor that gives the movement its reason to exist.[109] Standing above the movement's rhetoric is the metaphorical Africa, encompassing and activating the quest for unity, security, and liberty. "Africa" signifies an escape from racial discrimination and an epitomized pride in heritage. The metaphor becomes the message.[110]

The aim of the rhetoric was psychological and physical return to Africa. Garvey could shout,

> The more I remember the sufferings of my fore-fathers, the more I remember the lynchings in the Southern States of America, the more I will fight on even though the battle seems doubtful. Tell me that I must turn back, and I laugh you to scorn. Go on! Go on! Climb ye the heights of liberty and cease not in well doing until you have planted the banner of the Red, the Black, and the Green on the hilltops of Africa.[111]

Emigration to Liberia (as opposed to colonization—a white man's solution), was the only answer to an obvious dilemma. Bishop Henry McNeal Turner argued that "there is no more doubt in my mind that we have ultimately to return to Africa than there is of the existence of God.[112] Garvey and Turner kept the fires of Back-to-Africa burning in the hearts of black Americans well into the twentieth century.

Despite African American interest in Africa, an exceedingly small number, compared with the hundreds of thousands who joined the movements, made the trip back to Africa. Between the years 1816 and 1940, probably no more than 25,000 blacks migrated to the continent. Bishop Turner lamented in 1895, during the height of his Back-to-Africa agitation, that while 2,500 blacks had been lynched in the United States in the past ten years, only 361 blacks had emigrated to Africa.[113] Thus, counting the work of the American Colonization Society from 1816 to 1845 to colonize Liberia and Sierra Leone, and Marcus Garvey's efforts during the first quarter of the twentieth century, there were not more than 25,000 emigrés in total. For many poor blacks seeking passage to Africa, without access to shipping lines, unable to raise the necessary money for their families, and harassed by some whites for desiring to leave, the psychological avenue was the only road to liberation.

All myths, and particularly myths developed and borrowed from experience, can be put to use in cultural analysis. The Return myth, moreover, is one of the significant motifs of the African American experience, and every effort to analyze the culture of African Americans must deal adequately with it. If the African's initial reaction to bondage in a strange land was a persistent search for a way to return, decades of servitude and generations of discrimination have only reinforced the myth's power.

Part 3 **The Liberation**

This section examines the search for an Afrocentric method that can serve as the basis for analysis and synthesis in African and African American discourse. Drawing on fundamental African concepts, we seek to explain the ultimate quest for harmony as the predominant aspiration of African American orature and literature.

The Search for an Afrocentric Method

Throughout this book, I have been arguing that all analysis is culturally centered and flows from ideological assumptions; this is the fundamental revelation of modern intellectual history. An Afrocentric method is concerned with establishing a world view about the writing and speaking of oppressed people. Current literary theories—phenomenology, hermeneutics, and structuralism, for example—cannot be applied, whole cloth, to African themes and subjects. Based as they are on Eurocentric philosophy, they fail to come to terms with fundamental cultural differences. Consequently, some authors have mistaken European agitation, manifested as a rhetorical reaction to social, religious, and political repression, with African protest discourse that seeks the removal of oppression. Repression presumes that the persecuted have certain rights; oppression is the denial of these rights and humanity.

The principal crisis with which the Afrocentric writer or speaker is concerned remains the political/cultural crisis with all of its attendant parts, economic and social. Indeed, the same themes spring to life in the revolutionary work of African American musicians, artists, and choreographers who challenge assumptions about the universality of Eurocentric concepts. We are on a pilgrimage to regain freedom; this is the predominant myth of our life.

It is my intention to examine the constituent elements in an Afrocentric discourse, particularly literature; demonstrate how these constituents differ from others; and suggest ways to turn this theory towards a critical method for perfecting African American discourse as a liberating word against all oppressive words. Therefore (as I have been doing) I will treat discourse, both spoken and written, as having essentially the same philosophical problem of perspective.

I recognize that most literary theory, like rhetorical theory, is essentially European. This is not a condemnation; it is rather a basis for understanding the role of an Afrocentric theory. I have argued so far that the rest of the world cannot abandon the theoretical and critical task to European writers who stand on various literary "peaks" as beacons for theory. Almost all of them, moreover, have seen from a male, Eurocentric angle, which, in their estimation, equals "universal," and have therefore negated—and where not negated, ignored—other perspectives. One finds this hostile silence in the writings of Northrop Frye, Ferdinand de Saussere, and de Man, as well as Jacques Derrida.

The European Vision

What has been the purpose of literary theory in the twentieth century? The aim has been to rescue the depravity of thought, the carnage of ruined dreams, and the death of vision engendered by the first and second great European wars, which were called world wars. Kenneth Burke saw literature in dramatistic terms, but drama for him was essentially a European affair. In the 1930s and 1940s, nothing stood so enormous in European consciousness as their wars and no evil was as threatening as Hitler. He shattered their vision of themselves as morally superior, though they retained his sense of Aryan intellectual superiority, masking it in the myths of German scientific heroics, which also were warped. Hitler dared to enslave twentieth-century white people. Europeans could understand the domination of India and Nigeria, but not of Poland and France. Their idea was to consolidate the basic Western view of the world. They were not concerned about, nor were they under obligation to be concerned about, oppressed peoples.

Thus, out of this concern with Western decline and degradation we see the rise of Husserl's phenomenology and Heidegger's hermeneutics, both inextricably absorbed in European culture, without reservation. Edmund Husserl's *The Crisis of European Sciences* drew from an ideological context where irrationalism flourished, and a bewildering array of sterile positivism appeared to scare the spirit out of European thought.[1] Although the major advances in European literary theory came during the first real European civil war, it was not to be the last development. This is not a casual point, because the second renaissance of European theory in the twentieth century came during and after the second international European war, when Northrop Frye and Roman Jakobson and Claude Lévi-Strauss were cutting their teeth on structuralist ideologies that hoped either to "totalize" all literary genres or to seize a text as an object in space, synchronically, apart from any polluting social or political facts. Indeed, this "miracle" is still tried, to little avail, in many corners of academic institutions as Eurocentric writers endeavor to "totalize" within a simple Western frame of reference. This becomes, in fact, an imposition, an aggressive attempt to dominate, and is therefore no totalization at all.

Sartre deals with this problem as a problem of analytical reason in his *Critique de la raison dialectique.*[2] He was among the earliest Western writers to understand the complications of traditional Western analysis. He opposes dialectical to analytical reason and claims that the transcendental materialists, those who believe that dialectical reason is merely an extension of analytical reason, do not understand that dialectical reason is "none other than the very movement of totalization."³ This is almost an African conceptualization as expressed by the Mande in the word *woron*, "to get to the essence" of conversation, art, song, ritual, or music. Thus, the Mande seek to *yere-wolo*, "to give birth to self," by finding the true essence. Sartre says that dialectical knowledge comes in the moment of totalization—not in a reflection of the moment, but in the process itself.⁴ He contends that the primary characteristic of the critical experience is that it goes on inside the totalization. While he admits that, in practice, this "should be the reflective experience of anyone," he quickly deepens his position by stating that "when I say that the experience must be *reflective*, I mean that it is no more distinguishable, in the singularity of its moments, from the totalization in process than the reflection is distinguishable from the human *praxis*."⁵

Of course, Sartre is challenged on this point by Western traditionalists such as Claude Lévi-Strauss. Although they proceed from a Marxist position, they claim that the ultimate goal of human sciences is not to constitute man but "to dissolve man."⁶ Such scholars, who believe that studying men is just like studying ants, Sartre called "aesthetes."⁷ Small-minded aesthetes represent a considerable influence in Western academic circles. In his attack on Sartre's *Critique*, Lévi-Strauss states the general position of such aesthetes and, in so doing, shows clearly the distinctions between views of reason:

> Sartre in fact becomes the prisoner of his cogito: Descartes made it possible to attain universality, but conditionally on remaining psychological and individual; by sociologizing the cogito, Sartre merely exchanges one prison for another. Each subject's group and period now take the place of timeless consciousness. Moreover, Sartre's view of the world and man has the narrowness which has been traditionally credited to closed societies. His insistence on tracing a distinction between the primitive and civilized with the aid of gratuitous contrasts reflects, in a

scarcely more subtle form, the fundamental opposition he postulates between myself and others. Yet there is little difference between the way in which this opposition is formulated in Sartre's work and the way it would have been formulated by a Melanesian savage.[8]

The fact that Sartre tries to escape the confusion he finds in traditional Western conceptual theory is to be applauded by those who seek not merely an extension of a Western way of knowing, but also the peculiar dimensions of other ways of knowing.

Other Ways of Knowing

A symbol "revolution" was initiated by the Civil Rights Movement of the '60s and maintained by campaigns against the Viet Nam war. There were, of course, problems of focus. We were articulating a perspective about education that was radical even as we argued that Black Studies was not simply the study of black people but the study of African people from an Afrocentric perspective. This movement was to inaugurate an entire system of thinking about social sciences and criticism, and pointed to the inherent problems of Eurocentric theory when applied to the black literary or rhetorical movements. The intrinsic problems in Western discourse theory were revealed as systemic because even those who were sympathetic to "civil rights" often used a Eurocentric framework to speak of "agitative rhetoric," "protest literature," and so forth, when we should never have forced ourselves to take that position. Thus, even in that situation the European center was assumed and the burden of proof rested with those called dissenters, dissidents, oppressed, the disturbers of myths. What the symbol revolution has attempted to show is that the hallowed concepts of Western thought—rationality, objectivity, progress—are inadequate to explain all of the ways of knowing.

As one of Western culture's chief ideals, objectivity has often protected social and literary theory from the scrutiny that would reveal how theory has often served the interests of the ruling classes. In this respect, it is like other disciplines that have been hewn out of the arts and sciences. Although the 1960s and 1970s brought the Yale deconstructionists—Paul de Man, J. Hillis Miller, Geoffrey Hartman, and others—the whole intellectual enterprise could not be divorced from its internal framework. (In this regard, the deconstructionists are like the Sierra Club in Kenya or the Red Cross in South Africa: their jobs depend on the mistakes of others. An imperial ideology creates the need for missionaries and Red Cross workers.)

More damaging still has been the inability of European thinkers, particularly of the neo-positivist or empiricist traditions, to see that human actions cannot be understood apart from the emotions, attitudes, and cultural definitions of a given context. The Afrocentric thinker understands that the interrelationship of knowledge with cosmology, society, religion, medicine, and traditions stands alongside the interactive metaphors of discourse as principal means of achieving a measure of knowledge about experience. The Afrocentrists insist on steering the minds of their readers and listeners in the direction of intellectual wholeness.

The Implications for Rhetoric

Rhetoric has its cultural character. Are not speakers and listeners, writers and audiences, separated in the European sense? The separation implies that the speaker seeks "available means" to persuade the listeners. There are therefore speaker and listener societies—a plethora of possibilities to keep the "oppressed" in their places and the oppressors in theirs. Like African American cultural style that seeks to have experience confirmed by the intuition of participants, the objective must be to open the door for intercultural audiences to affirm discourse.

Baraka once understood this necessary insistence. In *Home*, he wrote that the solution to our problems will come from what he calls "Black National Consciousness." "If we feel differently, we have different ideas," he wrote.[9] As science and method combined, Afrocentricity became the rationalization of the alternative consciousness. The protectors of the basest Eurocentric theory, with its racist focus, describe their ethos as the universal ethos, encompassing the only correct view. There are few caveats in their writing; they do not see the narrowness of their own visions. If African American theory follows the same path, what would happen to progressive theory? Would we not be adding to the body of Eurocentric literature and thereby further isolating ourselves from the rest of humanity? Should not other views claim their rightful places alongside Eurocentric analysis? Furthermore, African Americans who participate only in Eurocentric views can easily become anti-black, the logical extension of European cultural imperialism. To be sure, there have been a host of African American critics and theorists who have added to African literature and orature; however, too many still see themselves as serving some artificial value to European scholarship. They are victims of their own identity crisis, a crisis produced purely by their submission to the roles whites have forced them to play.

How can the oppressed use the same theories as the oppressors? Is it possible that established European theory regards its view as the best way to understand the literature of African Americans? The decline in the number of universities offering courses in African American literary criticism since the 1960s demonstrates the disregard and low esteem the Eurocentric tradition holds for the assertions of change. This is clearly seen in the response of those in rhetoric and oratory.

Eurocentric critics cannot neutralize their cultural "superiority" when they criticize previous white critics or engage in criticism themselves. The deconstructionists come close to redesigning the critical framework, although much of what they do falls squarely within the context of the Eurocentric theoretical framework. So the fundamental question of ethno-centricism is never touched. In fact, the Eurocentric writers, both black and white, often try to consolidate their Euro-centric impositions. Their attempts at criticizing ethnocen-tric rhetoric never go beyond, nor can they go beyond, the limits of Eurocentricism. The writer who includes in a dis-course the statement that "children act like a bunch of wild Indians" may be criticized by these Eurocentric critics, but for the wrong reasons. They may find logic inconsistent, poor style (according to the norms), semantics imprecise, or other stylistic problems; but they seldom criticize such a speaker or writer for Eurocentric statements as such. They participate in the same Eurocentric thinking as the writer and can only dis-tance themselves in the mechanics of discourse, not the philo-sophical framework. Let us look at how this is played out in the field of spoken communication, rhetorical discourse.

Rhetoric's problem, and our problem with it, is both his-torical and systemic. Consider the Egyptian book *The Coming Forth by Day*, called in the West *The Book of the Dead*, which contained the earliest extant examples of public discourse, gave us the forms for salutatory introductions, and became a model for the writers of the Torah, the Koran, and probably the Bhagavad-Gita. From Africa, the seat of the oldest orga-nized civilizations as well as the birthplace of humanity, rhe-torical models and interest travelled across the sea to Sicily, Greece, and Rome. The rise of Egypt and Nubia, its mother, is conservatively put at 5,000 years before the rise of Greek civi-lization. Greek students had studied in Africa even prior to the matriculation of Socrates and Plato at the temples. Only a few writers have acknowledged the African origins, although Africa is the region where spoken and written arts are known to have begun. The neglect of African origins and contribu-tions to the world's intellectual history in effect misrepresents much knowledge and perpetuates a narrow scholarship. I make this point because rhetoric is grounded in the politics and culture of societies. A provincial, ethnocentric, xenopho-bic view of the world constitutes a serious problem for multi-cultural realities.

If we examine the flow of rhetoric in Western thought, we will see that even when the rhetorician poses as a critic in the interests of the oppressed, that critic seems incapable of the divestment of Eurocentric views. Criticism becomes criticism within a Eurocentric context, a sort of ruthless intellectual game in which scores are kept but the oppressed are not even represented. Invariably, rhetoric allies itself with the socio-economic (though not necessarily numerically) dominant culture. Therefore, the dilemma of the scholar who would break out of these restricting chains is fundamentally an ideological one. That is why John Henrik Clarke says that when Europeans colonized the world, they colonized information about it. Ngugi wa Thiong'o, the Kenyan novelist, has argued that the imposition of the European languages on Africans furthers the oppression of the people because their chances for mental liberation become remote. He says that the intended results of this mental colonization is despair, despondency, and a collective death-wish.[10]

Rhetoric must transcend ideologies, whether political or racial, in order to perform the task of continuous reconciliation. Even now, when the demise of the old rhetoric has been proclaimed for at least a quarter of a century, the "white" journals still publish tribe rhetoric, rhetoric that can have meaning in its theoretical content only to one group of people. Thus, many blacks are forced by economic considerations to "go Eurocentric." When all is added up, you get a grand total of pure, whited-out blacks who have fallen into the I-want-whites-to-accept-me trap, and even if they say "Accept me as I am," they mean "as I become whiter."

European cultural referents and Western expansionism are the twin towers of contemporary literary theory—a profound problem that cannot be solved merely by consciousness to themes, for example, black writers, minority communication, Native American, Asian, Mexican, or Puerto Rican creators of discourse. It deserves an architectonic treatment, a total reclamation of philosophical ground. What is needed is a true overarching framework for understanding and practicing literature and rhetoric; not a dictatorial rhetoric but the emergence of parallel frames of reference; the rise of free spirits and the setting straight of a new Ogunic pantheon in America and the world. This would mean the legitimacy of criticism based upon a plurality of cultural views. Universality can only be dreamed about when we have slept on truth based on specific cultural experiences. Isaac Bashevis Singer was asked, after he received the Nobel Prize for Literature, why he had always written about ghosts in Yiddish. He replied, "Are there any other type of ghosts?" This is the posture of a writer who affirms a world view. What can we suggest for ways to approach literature and orature?

Defining Afrocentric Discourse

I suggest three fundamental Afrocentric themes of transcendent discourse: (1) human relations, (2) humans' relationship to the supernatural, and (3) humans' relationships to their own being. In any culture and under any conceivable circumstances, these would be the areas of discourse that occur to me. To posit these three general themes is to try to diffuse some of the specific issues that occur as "universals" in contemporary analyses. Almost all knowledge has cultural relevance and must be examined for its particular focus. Cultural differences do exist and must be explained by perspective in any discussion of themes. Take the Ebonics example in language, "Got no money," or the fact that guilt and innocence elicit different responses in whites and blacks. There needs to be more cultural data to give us something like a literary and oratory file.

Again, take oratory as an example. Communicationists, who are as parochial as literary theorists and critics, know British and American speakers, but are generally ignorant of the speeches in other cultures. As we have said, the decline in the number of universities offering courses in African American literary criticism since the 1960s may demonstrate the disregard and low esteem the Eurocentric tradition holds for the assertions of change. This is clearly seen in the response of those in rhetoric and oratory. Increasingly, students obtain degrees without ever looking at an African discourse or conversation analytically. They are, therefore, often ignorant of the discourse cultures of others.

Certain Afrocentric assumptions are necessary when we approach the discussion of African American discourse, both in its theory and its criticism. First, we assume that the objective of such discourse, in the large, is the successful presentation of one of the three principal themes, often within the context of resistance to oppression, liberation from stereotypes, and action in anticipation of reaction. Secondly, we assume that the discourse conforms to certain elementary materials of our corpus of culture; this would suggest stylistic and argumentative features as well. Thirdly, we assume that the discourse is directed principally towards either a black, a non-black, or a mixed audience. Furthermore, we assume that the discourse will have certain adjustment features to various audiences.

Since so much of African American discourse, in the sense of people speaking and writing, occurs within a Eurocentric context, it is necessary to isolate those aspects of a critical theory, derived from the condition, that are applicable to discourse. The assumptions serve as emblematic stools upon which to rest the critical case. You cannot rightly call any African American discourse, merely because it is uttered by a black person, *Afrocentric*. In fact, donning the *agbada* of a critic, I believe that much so-called "black discourse" is essentially white or Eurocentric discourse by black people. A black person's writing does not make the writing Afrocentric, no more than living in Africa makes a person Afrocentric.

Carlton and Barbara Molette's *Black Theatre: Premise and Presentation* is the first genuinely Afrocentric discussion of the black American theater.[11] They establish a method for examining African American theater and, in so doing, demonstrate that space is unified in the Afrocentric ideal. In Eurocentric theater, aesthetic distance is maintained between actor and audience; in Afrocentric theater, there is no attempt to manipulate empathy by separation. It goes without saying that a lot of black theater is not Afrocentric.[12] If a cultural analyst begins with Sophocles rather than African ritual drama, he can only end with the separation of actors and audiences. Afrocentrically, we must say that such a conclusion is only one way to reach success, whether in drama or rhetorical discourse.

Speaking about black issues does not make a discourse Afrocentric. Perhaps there is a cruel hoax being played out in the context of our Western experience. We are often victims of assumptions that support the established value systems and critical theories with little regard to our own profound historical experiences. Among those experiences are the achievements of transcendence against great odds; furthermore, rhythm has been the way to that connection with the cosmic. A truly Afrocentric rhetoric must oppose the negation in Western culture; it is combative, antagonistic, and wholly committed to the propagation of a more humanistic vision of the world. Its foundation is necessarily the slave narrative. Its rhythms are harmonious, discordant only to those who have refused to accept either the truth of themselves or the possibility of other frames of reference. Afrocentric rhetoric, while it is in opposition to the negative in Western culture, allows other cultures to co-exist, and in that particular aspect is substantially different from Western rhetoric. It is neither imperialistic nor oppressive. Therein lies its invigorating power. While beauty is artifactual for the Western world, it is dynamic in the Afrocentric sense. Expression itself can be beautiful to the Afrocentric critic. Thus rhetoric is a transforming power, a mythic discourse in the midst of a plethora of symbols.

Furthermore, it does not secure its efficacy or originality in the same manner as Western discourse, perhaps because it does not force the same separations as Eurocentric lines of argument. Foucault points out that "the reason-madness nexus constitutes for western culture one of the dimensions of its originality."[13] In effect, Foucault says, from Bosch to Shakespeare to Nietzsche and the Western poets and musicians of the nineteenth and twentieth centuries, the threads of madness exist in the cultural fabric.[14] This is not the case with Afrocentric approaches to knowledge and knowing. A more circular system of thought is implied in Afrocentric rhetoric, one with numerous elements united in a grand movement towards freedom of the mind, the irrepressible will to harmony.

Daniel and Smitherman's essay on deep structures within black communication behavior gave currency to the notion of generative, intangible, subjective ideas of a culture.[15] For them, the centrality of religion would constitute a deep structure, revealed through song, worship, and other "surface" features of our communicative behavior. Their emphasis is on the behavioral expressions of people who have shared a common experience. There is validity in this concept.

But this concept alone does not provide us a valid basis for the criticism of orature, except where we listen to the *pathos* of our spirit and comment on the uniqueness of that quality. It is, however, limiting in a pan-African sense, inasmuch as all African peoples have not experienced the same set of oppressive conditions as the Africans of the Americas. I possess all the pathos of the slaveships, the cotton fields, the spit in the face, the segregation, and the multitude of miniviolences in deed, and word-violences found in the Americas, and yet I do not find the same pathos in the voice of my brother from Mali or my sister from Kenya. In the Cuban, the Jamaican, the Brazilian, the Columbian, the Barbadian, the Haitian, the Trinidadian—yes, I recognize what Leon Phillips calls the "cadences and tonal variations that energize, envelop, and stir audiences to communal synthesis."[16] These are people who have had similar oppressive experiences. On the other hand, a critical method should account for more than presentational styles. Delivery is a fundamental constituent of discourse criticism, to be sure, but it is even more difficult than I first realized to generalize beyond certain geo-social and eco-cultural groups.

My intention is more comprehensive: I seek a critical method applicable to Africans, wherever they are, in much the same way Western scholars have set the procedures for criticizing Western discourse. Therefore, although I am interested in the centrality of religion and other "deep structures," I have chosen to concentrate my critical attention on an Afrocentric perspective to the world. How does the speaker view the world? To what end does he speak? Are his symbols discordant or harmonious? Does he demonstrate the currency of his ideas within the context of sanity? These are questions that must be addressed to every African who attempts discourse.

The *etic* and *emic* debate constitutes one way of viewing the challenge I have set. Etic approaches to criticism are those methods that are from *outside* the discourse perspective, whereas the emic approach, which views the perspective from within, is criticism derived from *within* the same culture as the discourse. What is proposed here is an emic criticism, derived from the culture, capable of speaking to the discourse in the language of the culture.

Albert Murray insists that it is necessary to see all statements as counterstatements, inasmuch as blacks in the United States possess a natural, historical, different view of reality than whites.[17] This calls into being the need for emic criticism, an internal understanding without the fault of Eurocentric social sciences, which assures a peculiar universality of European views. Murray contends that "the one place U.S. negroes [sic] have always found themselves most rigidly segregated is not in the inner sanctum of the is-white family but in the insistent categories of behavioral science surveys, studies, and statistics."[18] Without sensitivity to the intellectual and cultural elements of others, the white social scientist has often proceeded as if what is correct for whites is correct for everybody.

In African philosophy there is a commitment to harmony that some might call spirituality.[19] It is the manifest essence of a search for resolution of cultural and human problems. This essence may be present in poetry, music, or dance. Duke Ellington, Martin Luther King Jr., and Malcolm X all possessed it. In spoken discourse, it is possible to choose spirituality, word power, and call-and-response as the principal constituents of a culture-sensitive African-base critical method. Yet it seems to me that a proper understanding of spirituality leads us to the conclusion that the discourse of the preacher is of the same genre as that in the good blues musician. The so-called culture-sensitive African-base approach begins to answer these questions better than the neo-Aristotelian, phenomenological, structuralism, or post-structuralism approach to criticism because it admits the possibility of other views. It is one more evidence that African intellectuals question the basis of Western rhetoric as applied to African discourse. We understand the limitations of literary and rhetorical theory in the West. Frye's four narrative categories, *comic*, *romantic*, *tragic*, and *ironic*, leave little room for African literature, where romance does not assume such a burden as in the West.

However, Afrocentricity is not merely cultural sensitivity. To be culturally sensitive, one may remain grounded in one's own particular plot of history and mythology. The Eurocentricist may be culturally sensitive to the Wolof custom of leavetaking without ever modifying the central ground. An Afrocentricist may express cultural sensitivity to the Malay greeting behavior. Cultural sensitivity should be valued and practiced, but that does not constitute a cohesive critical direction for a body of discourse. This is why the attempt to define the scope of the concept *Afrocentricity* is important for the development of a more robust theoretical discussion.

The Link Between Black Studies and an Afrocentric Paradigm

Since the 1960s cultural sensitivity has been confused with the movement to establish Black Studies as an academic pursuit. Black Studies programs (rarely were they privileged with department status) sprouted all over the country, but many traditionalists simply regarded them as places where Black students could build self-esteem and study the achievements of Black writers. The conceptual underpinnings of the movement—the idea that it grew from a unique perspective as well as a coherent culture—were denied. As the key figures in the Black Studies movement, Maulana Karenga, James Turner, and James Stewart have held the front line in the debates about the place of Black Studies in academe.[20]

While recognizing their contributions, I would contend that what Stewart and Karenga view as difficulties in developing a paradigm in African American Studies are not any more significant than problems one encounters in any community or social or human science. Stewart identifies three factors that hinder a Black Studies program: the interdisciplinary nature of Black Studies, the dual nature of scholarship, and *praxis,* and the tendency to assume Black Studies' origins as a discipline in the 1960s, which denies its longer history.[21] These factors represent interesting but not authentic departures for a discussion of the problematics of the discipline of Black Studies. I find Karenga's support of Stewart's concerns troublesome.[22] While both Stewart and Karenga make valuable contributions to the general study of this field, they have not adequately assessed the nature of Afrocentric theory as the *sine qua non* of Black Studies. Let us examine Stewart's three factors more closely.

First, the fact that Black Studies is interdisciplinary should present no more difficulty for it than such nature presents for sociology, political science, economics, or geography; all are essentially interdisciplinary or multidisciplinary. The creation of a paradigm or the codification of substantive theories and procedures does not depend on singular study of a discipline. In fact, the idea of discipline, inherited from the German School, has little to do with an intellectual enterprise in the twentieth century. The abandonment of this archaic notion has been coming for a long time. Therefore, the fact that Black Studies deals with many subjects is no hindrance to the flowering of an Afrocentric paradigm.[23] Afrocentricity, in recognizing the centrality of a world view based on Africa, "finds its place in the origins of civilization as well as in every compartment of post-modern history."[24] The advancement of the African American Studies paradigm must begin with a codified Afrocentricity, that is, a regularized and orderly arrangement of procedures for inquiry, analysis, and synthesis. Of course, codification must be undertaken on what already exists; once we have the proper grammar, based on what exists, we will be more comfortable with the perspective, now transformed into method and science, regardless of the subject or theme under study.

Stewart's second factor deals with the fact that African American Studies must contain both scholarship and *praxis*. This is a dubious bifurcation. Afrocentric scholarship is itself *praxis*. Afrocentricity as paradigm has propaedeutic value because a myriad of assumptions and basic propositions employed by African American Studies can be examined. Such scholarship as *praxis* reduces the tendency for individuals to make random, non-connected comments, even though those comments might be informative. The logic of procedure provides groundwork for others to follow; this is the value of Afrocentric scholarship as work. I am not convinced that either Stewart or Karenga believes that Afrocentric scholarship is not *praxis*. What Stewart had in mind was, perhaps, a more pedestrian interpretation of *praxis*. Needless to say, this should not be seen as a difficulty in establishing a paradigm.

Finally, Stewart's statement that the tendency to assume Black Studies originated in the 1960s is a problem; in my view, such a tendency does not disconnect the field from its longer history, as he contends. Although African people have been studied prior to the revolutionary paradigmatic changes of the 1960s, I suggest that the origins of African American Studies are in that era. Thus, while stating that Stewart's three factors "were correctly focused and well founded," Karenga challenges this last factor by saying "as an *academic discipline* . . . Black Studies did begin in the 1960s."[25] This position is in keeping with my contention that African American Studies must be defined not by subjects or themes, but by an Afrocentric perspective that is central to the paradigm.

Perhaps Karenga was merely attesting to the value of Stewart's conceptualization to a continuing heuristic.

James Turner, the founder of the Africana Research Center at Cornell University, argues in support of James Stewart's thesis that Black Studies originated prior to the 1960s. Citing Carter G. Woodson, the father of African American history, as an early proponent of Black Studies, Turner writes,

> Black Studies as a field of scholarship did not begin with the student turmoil of the late sixties. Men and women have, for many years, studied and written about African American history, literature, and art. A small number of scholars have, for a long time, engaged in critiques of American society from the perspectives of Black Americans. An important fact about these early scholarly endeavors is that they occurred almost entirely at Black colleges or universities or outside the higher education setting altogether. When the late Carter G. Woodson, a pioneer in African American history, observed that the whole system of education in America conspires to teach Black people to despise themselves, he was referring to the characteristic of the white-dominated education system that almost wholly excluded consideration of Blacks in the history, culture, and economic life of America.[26]

Both Stewart and Turner overstate the case. Woodson, to use Turner's example, was first and foremost a proponent of history, and not of the field of African American Studies; and if he understood history as the sum total of the field, it was a misunderstanding. What we see in the 1960s is the coalescence of Afrocentricity in every compartment of human endeavor; this is the exceptional fact of the creation of the field.

There are several functions that make an Afrocentric paradigm necessary for the advancement of the field of African Studies. The first is the grammar or notational function, which gives a concise base to principal concepts and ideas. Secondly, paradigms make it possible to trace the logical development of arguments because they derive from clear components of the paradigm. Thirdly, paradigms allow us to build upon previous foundations. For example, Afrocentricity becomes a school of thought, a paradigm, based upon work since the 1960s. Fourthly, an Afrocentric paradigm promotes analysis and synthesis rather than mere description. Attention to these functions makes it possible to have a powerful theoretical perspective for examining any branch of human science.

Elements of Criticism

How do we turn this theoretical perspective towards a critical method? Or should we propose a critical method at all? Is not criticism itself a fundamental category of Western education? Perhaps a more basic question for us is, What function is served by criticism? The aim of criticism is to pass judgment, and judgment is concerned with good and bad, right and wrong; criticism is, therefore, preeminently an ethical act. One may appropriate other qualities to the critical act, but it is essentially a judgment. The Afrocentric critic is also concerned with ethical judgments but finds the aesthetic judgment equally valuable, particularly as the substantial ground upon which to make a decision about the restoration of harmony and balance. Indeed, Afrocentric criticism essentially combines ethics and aesthetics. If we were to examine the aims of oratory according to Western critics, we would typically be drawn to instruction, persuasion, and entertainment. However, these distinctive ends of oratory or literature—as far as that goes—are tied to the goal of influencing people to accept a certain view of reality. The commercialization of the word becomes the chief end of language and what it takes to "get over" the primary driving force.

In an Afrocentric conception of literature and orature, the critical method would be employed to determine to what degree the writer or speaker contributed to the unity of the symbols, the elimination of chaos, the making of peace among disparate views, and the creation of an opportunity for harmony and hence balance. Let me explain further: Harmony, in the sense that I am speaking of it, is an equilibrium among the various factors impinging upon communication.

One sees the difference between an African conception of rhetoric and, say, that of Kenneth Burke. Burke's dramatistic conception is based on a view of human beings as symbol users who often have to be brought together to overcome differences, to persuade. It seems to me that the African pattern as described, for example, in one cultural part of Africa, the Shona, is quite different in that all human beings are a part of an organic whole, and it is not so much the persuasion that implies estrangement as it is the restoration of balance that matters when one speaks. The critic, therefore, must see to what extent the speaker achieved this purpose.

What are the tools of the critic? Since Afrocentric theory is based upon a cultural and historic perspective, the critic must understand both the cultural and historical bases of the discourse. The critic maintains an empathic engagement with the audience of a writer in order to properly understand how the writer creates or re-creates harmony in audiences. This empathic engagement allows the critic to participate in the event as well as to assess it.

Such a position, of course, is radical empiricism, maintaining that the subjective analysis of data is the most humanistic and correct critical approach to works meant for human audiences. But the critic must ensure that his or her judgment, subjective as it must be, is grounded in the historical and cultural bases of the discourse. One cannot use the Afrocentric critical method if one is ignorant of cultural and historical bases. Attempting to do so would lead to gross errors in judging whether or not a writer has achieved harmony within an audience. To evaluate a piece about Ethiopia, one must know something about Ethiopia; to proceed otherwise would not be Afrocentric. It may be phenomenological. But phenomenological approaches to African culture, based on Eurocentric perspectives, lead to incorrect conclusions.

For example, the writer who wishes to write about African communication, either in the Americas or in Africa, must be familiar with cultural styles. Otherwise the writer will assume that words, even words of a European language, are used in a European manner. We know, of course, that no mere word contains an idea, concept, or thought. The word must first be designated by the verbal expression of a person. Apart from the tonal elements in some African languages, there is immediate meaning to a word, perhaps even several meanings to a word, before one can grasp its meaning. "Bad" may mean evil or good, or something else, depending on the speaker. In this sense, a word may be a tightly contracted sentence, made so by several elisions. I can say "my" as an expression of joy-satisfaction at someone beautiful and express several sentences in that word. I do not imply that such capability is unknown in any other cultures; I simply argue that it is a facility in African culture that must be taken into consideration when making an analysis. Words in this type of context do not become clichés because they are constantly re-energized and re-interpreted.

Harmony has been achieved when the audience says a collective "amen" to a discourse, either through vocal or symbolic acknowledgment. This does not imply that logic has been achieved or that factual information has been presented, though these aspects are most likely present in the discourse when harmony is achieved. However, perceived logic or perceived facts are good enough to achieve harmony. The critic must assess whether the audience experienced harmony or not, to what degree harmony was achieved, and how the speaker handled the major obstacles to harmony. Forensic essays may or may not contribute to harmony, but they should move in that direction. In these cases, the critic wants to analyze what type of problems existed that impeded or facilitated harmony. Could they have been overcome by the writer (or writers) *without* losing integrity? (By "integrity" is meant the attachment to an Afrocentric reality and vision.) If the only way to achieve "harmony" is through divesting a person's cultural and historical bases, then it is an achievement that is without rhetorical merit. It has merit only as demagoguery, because the discourser's aim becomes the achievement of a *product,* regardless of cost. In a sense, it is an exploitation of the readers or audiences.

This critical method, applied to Afrocentric discourse, succeeds in presenting a positive rather than a reactionary posture to discourse. When it is used to assess African American writers, it could be considered a severe method because it would expose in those speakers the lack of an Afrocentric consciousness, much as Marxist method would expose the rhetoric of Abraham Lincoln, Daniel Webster, and Ronald Reagan as reflecting class-interests. This is not to say that black writers could not receive "positive" points on many aspects of their discourse, but it *is* to say that they would not automatically be adjudged great by this method—whereas if one applied any of the critical methods developed in a Eurocentric context, several black writers may be outstanding writers. These are hard questions that will be worked on for years. Is it fair to criticize an Afrocentric writer from a Eurocentric perspective?

I do not castigate any other method, for all methods are valid within their contexts. Initially, I said that analysis is culturally centered; likewise, critical methods flow from some ideological commitment. Truly to understand and appreciate the dilemma of African American and African writers trained in the West, one has to study discourse from an Afrocentric perspective. This, therefore, is a continuation of a literary and rhetorical quest for the theoretical and critical equilibrium necessary for placing African American discourse in its proper place. What is true of discourse is also true of other forms of human activity—transcendence, for example. Transcendence, the quality of exceeding ordinary and literal experience, occurs in the African's response to nature and relationships, when personal and collective harmony is achieved. It is, of course, linked to cultural factors, and any discussion of how people transcend or discuss their transcendence must consider the historical and cultural experiences that constitute their existence. In the next section, I shall turn to what Dona Richards has called the "spiritual reality" of the African person in response to circumstances and environment.

Transcendence:
The Curved Line

A Dilemma of Thought

I have been dealing so far with the abiding dilemma in Western formulations, of all sciences and arts, with the problem of self-aggrandizement. Even in its reach for diversity, a Western philosophy or science creates, *inter alia*, limitations. In the West, one may tolerate diversity of viewpoints and then establish a single set of criteria for what constitutes validity. In this formulation, neither African nor Southern Hemisphere thought amounts to much. This is not merely ignorance in the sense of ignoring the ways in which people in the cradle of humanity and civilization have dealt with communications or transcendence; it is, more seriously, the continuation of Western imposition of a view of the world, and the assumption that it is real. The problem is not in the expounding of Western categories but in the absolute manner in which they are assumed to constitute the whole of human thought. This is unacceptable, in any field, on intellectual and cultural grounds.

I have argued for an Afrocentric perspective on literature and orature, and by extension there is reason to make this argument in transcendence. "How we got ovah" is an explosive, galactic expression, full of wonder and power, because the meaning is transcendence, whether in the personal, social, political, geographical, economic, or spiritual sense. Contained in its tight construction are all of the sentiments found in good literature or orature. In effect, it is the perfect transcendent declaration, the generative, productive *nommo*, finally and emphatically made real.

A powerful, expressive modality allows Westerners and, increasingly, Asians to speak of the great religions and mean by such an expression Buddhism, Christianity, Islam, and Judaism. Indeed, the great religious thinkers become Buddha, Jesus, Mohammed, and Moses. I do not know what constitutes their greatness—that is, any more than the greatness, say, of Oduduwa of the Yoruba, Okomfo of the Asante, or Chaminuka of the Shona. The West has religions of literature, as opposed to orature; perhaps the individuality of their leaders inheres in this fact. They are also one-god religions, and although I must confess my intellectual bias against the imperialism that comes out of one-god religions, I can see how that fact might score in the minds of Westerners. And yet this is not enough to explain the omission of Africa from the discussion of human transcendence, since most African religions also express a one-god ideology. When the way to transcendence is found in peoples' lives as they deify their own nationalism and history, that becomes sufficiency and greatness for them.[27]

Human civilization began in the Nile Valley with the gifts of Nubia. The temples of Karnak and Luxor held secrets of the mysteries, which have been explored by Schwaller de Lubicz, Ben-Jochannan, Budge, Diop, and others in great detail. The ancient mysteries contained in the books of the great priests of the holy lodges held the key to African transcendence nearly five thousand years before the Arab *jihads* swept out of Arabia and conquered Northern Africa, stamping out, for the most part, the indigenous Egyptian language and establishing Islam as religion and Arabic as language. The subsequent dispersal of the secret societies to various other places on the African continent made it possible for the re-emergence of these secrets in the Yoruba Ifa, the Shona Mbira, and the Asante Okyeame system, among other traditions. These oral traditions have demonstrated the integration of African medicine, theology, and agriculture.

Jahn says, in *Muntu*, that no traditional African ever thinks of medicine not connected to religion, to agriculture, to nature, to the village. This wholism is uniform and unbroken. Of course, one could see, as Jahn does, the enormous psychological pressure on Westernized Africans, yet somewhere there remains, even in the most Westernized African, a sense of this harmony.[28] As I have intimated, in the West one can be an atheist and believe in science or medicine; this is impossible in the Sudic ideology. That is why the African American, as a new African ethnic group, brings a unique relationship to the concept of transcendence. Whether you are speaking of the Brazilian, Jamaican, Cuban, Haitian, or United States African, they all share the same experience or forms of the experience: Samba, Sango, Candomble, Santeira, Voodoo, Macumba, Umbanda, and Mial. At the center of all of these forms of human expression is the same source of energy. They operate on the rhythms of orality. The African person, seeking tranquility and transcendence, finds it in the traditions of human expression developed in the context of African philosophy and myth.

In Ifa divination among the Yoruba, the idea is always to restore harmony. Wande Abimbola says, in *Ifa Divination Poetry*, that when Ifa left the earth and returned to heaven, the earth was thrown into chaos and confusion.[29] He writes that "human society moved dangerously close to anarchy and disorder as everything was faced with imminent destruction."[30] The following poem suggests the situation:

> Pregnant women could not deliver their babies,
> Barren women remained barren.
> Small rivers were covered with fallen leaves.
> Semen dried up in men's testicles,
> Women no longer saw their menstruation.
> Yam formed small but undeveloped tubers;
> Corn grew small but unripened ears.
> Scattered drops of rain fell down,

> Chicken attempted to eat them up:
> Well-sharpened razors were placed on the floor,
> And goats attempted to devour them.[31]

Ifa's children tried to persuade him to return to earth, in order that peace might return. Instead, Ifa gave his children sixteen palmnuts, and those palmnuts became the most important instruments in Ifa divination. Harmony and peace, societal and individual, come from the right ordering of the earth through an appeal to Ifa.

One would certainly find it difficult to understand much of contemporary Africa without an Afrocentric appreciation of context. There is a relationship of community with the enviro-technical, as well as the ancestral, world.

The Romans believed in the existence of *numen*, the mystical power the gods gave to some people and withheld from others. This power raised those so favored to the status of kings, noble people, and philosophers. Those so favored, those with *numen*, were distinguished from those who did not have *numen*. In other words, the people of God received the grace that was dished out selectively. The people fulfilled themselves in the perpetual conflict between the principles of good and evil. This gave to their life on earth the character of a dialectical process; they were forever buffeted between the forces of good and evil. Of course, one could strike a *quid pro quo* bargain with *numen* and thus secure favor.

I like to call the product of this the *bias of categorization*, which divides people into teachers and those taught, sinners and saved, black and white, superior and inferior, weak and strong. Out of this bias has developed the catastrophic disharmonies that we experience in the world. Cycles within cycles, wheels within wheels of contradiction, which no amount of what the servants of god called *mysteries* could resolve, have been the inevitable results. Opposed to the bias of categorization is the wholistic view found in the traditional African world view.

The African American view of a wholistic personality, which is the healthy person, is grounded in the African idea of *sudicism*, the spiritual commitment to an ideological view of harmony. In the African American view, the person must be harmonized, because an undisciplined person creates disharmony within the society. It is the quest for harmony that is at the source of all literary, rhetorical, or behavioral actions; the *sudic* ideal, which emphasizes the primacy of the person, can only function if the person seeks individual and collective harmony. But this is not all. One must understand that to become human, to realize the promise of becoming human, is the only important task of the person. One becomes human only in the midst of others. The person is defined as human by his or her actions that lead to harmony; our attitude towards this person gives the dynamism necessary to produce a harmonized personality. This is why the black church exudes a collective sense of harmony.

Really to understand this, you must know that the African world does not recognize external forces that aid in producing this self-definition of a person. The person does not look for external powers; those powers inhere in him as an extension into the future of those who have gone before; he is a testament to his forebears in a different guise, living in a different period. When I summon these inherent powers, I know that I am indebted to no power outside myself. In a transpersonal sense, the more I recognize and develop my powers, the more human I become. I am in tune with the rhythm of the universe. Since transcendence is, in the end, the regulation of this harmonious power, we become seekers of the type of connections, interactions, and meetings that lead to harmony. I am most healthy when I am harmonized with others. I am most in touch with transcendence when I am moving in time to others.

Now here is the point. There is no end to this challenge of becoming a person because there is no end to seeking harmony. When we go within ourselves—that is, when we turn inward to explore the eternal reality that holds the secrets of the person—we find that one may go on forever in this way, that no one can give you these dimensions, these new dimensions, and nobody can take them away. You find them, we say, in your eternal quest for harmony and, by so doing, you become more human as the master of your own powers, but always in the midst of others. Such is the essence of the oral tradition's influence on all African expression.

Personalism and Collective Power

There are essentially three major paradigms that govern how we understand phenomena. In one way, we assume that all that we see, all that we feel, all that exists as matter is an illusion, so we seek what many call the *spiritual dimension* of reality, of ourselves, of our lives, of our environment, even of our colleagues. We might say, It is not your body but your spirit that attracts me. Of course, that is putting it at one particular level; nevertheless, the same paradigm is operating, the search for the answer beyond the material.

Another fundamental paradigm in Western thought is based on the logical positivist tradition that says, Show me the "real" thing—the facts, the evidence, the "hard" data; only if I can touch it, smell it, feel it, taste it, or see it, is it real. So if I tell such a person that a certain musician has soul, he wants me to demonstrate it in the laboratory, to identify it statistically, to measure it. This paradigm sees everything that is not concrete, that is not material, as an illusion, a misplaced dream.

Then there is the paradigm that answers the questions of the most intense moments of crisis with the *sudic* ideal, *personalism*, which is itself an ideal ideological commitment to harmony, and the fundamental Afrocentric response to phenomena. Personalism finds its strength in the idea that anything we want to happen can happen if we are committed to following the lead of *nommo*, the generative quality of the spoken word. Neither spiritualism nor materialism is anything without the person. The person is the marker, the tagger for what is real. Thus, the fact that the Zulu can cause their hearts to stop beating at will for a few minutes does not introduce any difficulty into the *sudic* ideal, because what the Zulu can do with their hearts the Asante and the Yoruba can do with theirs, and vice versa. Some can step on fire and not be burned, some have planted swords into the earth that cannot be pulled out by a human; and yet all of this is nothing. The only thing that really matters is the person. That is why the drummer goes to recite incantation to the trees before he cuts them down to make his drums; that is why the people of Niger always stalk a lion with words of praise and incantations before they shoot it; and that is why the lion, after it is shot, lies down and dies peacefully, according to the incantation of the person.

There is nothing to the spiritual, nor to the material, that is not activated by the person. So I can say that personalism, in the African and African American sense, is neither spiritualism nor materialism, but the activating energy contained in the person.

Releasing the energy in the person is done by various libations and rituals. Each person contains these energies; some cultivate them more than others, but they inhere in all of us. But how does one go about finding these energies, these essences of personalism? How can they be located? What pathway leads to the infinite ability to make material and spiritual what we desire them to be?

To find an answer to these questions, there are several things that you must know about African American transcendence. The African finds energy and life in the midst of persons; he or she does not escape to mountains, or the valleys, or the seashores in order to find the energy. There is no "great tradition" of withdrawal in the African or African American tradition; ours is preeminently a tradition of remarkable encountering with others. But encountering, for us, is always accompanied by words and, as such, it is profoundly verbal. Hermits rarely exist and all would-be Thoreaus are "baptized" in the fires of human excitement, because it is only in the give and take of the *nommo* that we find energy, not in the lives of solitude. There is some belief that hermeticism results from suspicion and distrust of persons other than one's self.

Again, we edge back to the Romans and *numen*. Nothing is more beautiful to me than the ecstasy that occurs when a group of people have got on the same road to harmony at the same moment; that is the true manifestation of spirituality, the true materiality of life, which can only be determined by the person joining in the collective expression of power.

This is one of the supreme legacies we have given to America. I am no longer myself, I am a transpersonal being at this moment of collective expression. I am feeling at the moment. It is not a left-brain moment, it is joy ineffable, because we are in tune with the feelings of others. I experience *nommo*, and I know that nothing can save me except the spoken word in the moment of collapse; but beyond that I am one with the orality of *nommo*, I exist in it and it exists in me. The printed page is "silent" compared to the spoken word. This is the message of both sacred and secular orators in the African American experience. Malcolm's rhetoric was meant to convey his audiences towards the ultimate goal of possession, that is, the attaining of harmony through style and power. Such is the truth of Martin Luther King Jr., Louis Farrakhan, and the words of Ogotommêli, the Dogon sage.

We stand together holding up the collapsing roof, and this is the most awesome knowledge confronting us. We handle this awesome knowledge by maturing in a collective sense. This is the secret of African American spirituality; that is, while we recognize the individuality of the responsibility, we know that it cannot be carried out without others. We can reach our *own* transcendence, but never without the help of others. If I run to the sea alone, my solitude finds me searching for new ways to come together with others. I know myself only in relation to others, without whom I am a Piagetian egocentric. We say that we can never truly know ourselves without the knowledge of others; or more precisely, in the productive engagement with the other we truly experience our own harmony. This is the *sudic* ideal.[32] Richards has expressed this goal as that of discovering the point of harmonious inter-action, so that interferences become neutralized, allowing constructive energy to flow and be received.[33] She further states that in Africa the "human is divine."[34]

When the black entertainers introduced the phrase "Put your hands together," it was not for the purpose of applause, as in the European hand clapping that is derived from the Germanic rattling of swords and spears in approval of a chief's speech. Rather, what they meant to do was to call an audience to a collective generative experience. Since the traditional performers and audiences in Africa were one, it was not far-fetched for the entertainers, especially singers, to call their audiences to these touching moments. Inherent in this rhythmic quality of touching hands together, of audiences caught up in collective expression, was the fundamental search for harmony.

Possession

It is this *nommo* quality that leads directly, if the person seeks transcendence, to "possession." Now possession is not the same as Gurdjieff self-remembering, or Krishnamurti self-knowledge, or Sufi concentration, or Raja Yoga concentration, though it is a way to enlightenment. Possession is almost always accompanied by music and incantation, whether vocal or instrumental. But you cannot achieve it alone; it is collective and is the result of "perfect harmony" with self, nature, and the universe. It is sense experience, a response to feeling; not so much a response to thought as a following of the rhythms of nature. I would not even go so far as to call it consciousness, because consciousness is not an entity but a process of attention; one cannot have consciousness unless one is conscious of something. That is why I can only say that in possession there are no unshared edges, no hanging questions, no impossible dreams at the moment of feeling. At that moment numbers merge into spirit, and we become transcendent. Clearly, we may reach the state of transcendence by many roads. Once it is reached we are no longer the same; we are compatriots with others who have crossed the chasm by various means.

It is by no means given that all will reach possession in this generative, productive way; some may never know the experience. But this is so with all ways to transcendence. We must still search in order to find. And those who are not in the search mode will never find. This is why I claim that the proper understanding of the African culture can only be achieved by looking through Afrocentric eyes.

All transpersonal moments are times of energy. That is why we often hear people speak of the possession experience in terms of work. They will say, "Boy, they worked themselves up," or "Girl, he worked himself into a frenzy." There is truth and error in these statements, because work is involved in the first instance; that is, you cannot have the transpersonal state promised by the African American mode of spirituality without energy being expended. On the other hand, we cannot possibly speak of one working herself or himself "up" or "into a frenzy." These terms have little significance and almost no meaning in the context of *nommo*. Possession is an individual state of harmony, usually reached in a collective experience of a rhythmic nature. As such, it is neither up nor down; perhaps it is "all around." It is not even necessary to say, lest we walk into the Roman trap of *numen* again and start saying whether up is better than possession. The experience matters. Harmony matters.

Possession is not the result of a trance, although trance has been associated wrongly with possession. I have heard people say, "Well, she was in a trance" or "He fell into a trance," referring to someone who had experienced the complete harmony of possession in the African American mode. A trance has little growth potential and may be the results of an accident or illness; possession, on the contrary, must be sought. Sometimes people will refer to a "trance-like" state in an attempt to be more precise about what they cannot explain. Nevertheless, "possession" is only explained in the sense of a person seeking to possess. A trance is basically a physiological state that may be caused by hypnotism or coma; possession is spiritual, although it is usually accompanied by physiological changes. It is a cleansing of the spirit and, as such, produces euphoria for the individual and a sense of peace for the collective others who witness the possession.

Furthermore, it is a mistake to assume that possession, in this context, means that the person is "being possessed." When Europeans first saw that collective ceremonies and rituals of rhythm produced the state of possession in some people, they interpreted it as the people being possessed. Even some African writers, particularly the Cubans and Brazilians, have written in this way about *candomble* and *umbanda*. To these observers, the person is "possessed" by the gods of Africa, mainly Yoruba, Shango, Legba, Yemanja, Ogun, and Obatala.

But this is incorrect; it is not the person who is being possessed, but the gods and goddesses. Therefore, the act of possession always starts as an act of volition on the part of the person, not on the part of the gods. The person possesses the "gods" through searching in the proper mode and finding harmony. Now to speak like this is not to speak wholly of what might be called a "church" experience, but rather to show that the person actively and creatively participates in his own Afrocentric experience.

Music as a Vehicle for Transcendence

What is more, the experience of "possession" has little to do with the church context, though it is visible there. What I mean is that the church is only one venue for the African American experience of this harmony. To be certain about things is one of the best environments, because so many of the necessary conditions are in the church. Yet the truth is that the feeling can be found wherever people are congregated and there is an ample amount of heavy rhythms. The work gangs in the South, during and after slavery, produced some of the most beautiful music in search of harmony with nature. Roland Hayes and Paul Robeson popularized the folk versions of the work songs in the early part of the twentieth century.

The contagion of popular music throughout the modern world is due to the heavy insistence of the incessant African rhythms that came to the vocabulary of music with the concept of *beat*, as in "beat on a drum." All the world is addicted to the music of "popular dance." This is a major African contribution to the directed energies of the world. Furthermore, even in its watered-down version it is a spiritual contribution without parallel. Since music and dance are never separated in the African context, the percussive beat, which "lifts" dancers, has become the mainstay of popular music of all varieties.

Since rhythm is a principal path to transcendence for the African American, further exploration of this dimension could lead to a transcendental awakening that might take into consideration certain aspects of transcendental realism of the sort proposed by Roy Bhaskar in *A Realist Theory of Science*.[35]

Bhaskar has taken on the whole of European theory in regard to science itself, proposing what he sees as an alternative to neo-positivism and phenomenology. He holds that the objective of science is explanation; one does not have to predict. In the view of Bhaskar, a reappraisal of both the neo-positivist and hermeneutic/phenomenology traditions will result in better understanding. While the phenomenologists do not suffer from the same rigidity as the empiricists, they do have the problem of insisting on empathetic understanding of a situation. The problem is that if the understanding is derived from a constrained Eurocentric view, one is likely to get an interpretation of Nat Turner that says he was insane. An Afrocentric critic could not find such an interpretation in the character; thus the outcry when William Styron published his novel. Nat Turner was nothing short of a conflict between an "empathetic" Eurocentricist and black readers.

The call-and-response mode is also important to our understanding of the experience. One can easily assume, when one listens to the experience, that it is the speaker calling and the audience responding. These roles, however, often shift, but most of the time the audience calls and the speaker responds, going as deep or as high as he can. It is this direct search for harmony that is at the base of African American spirituality. We seek it everywhere and all of the time, and then there are those moments when it bursts full blown into our souls and we take wings and fly for a while.

The graceful basketball player, who moves in tune to the rhythms of the game in just such a way as to bring his body in harmony with the particular moment of decision on the court, is in search of the experience. The football player, who eludes several other players in his quest to make a touchdown, knows that to have done it well is not enough; one must do it in such a manner that harmony is served. You must make it look easy, fluid, natural, inevitable. In the end, the experience is made to seem predictable. This is the function of rhythm, this is the achievement of enlightenment. As with the old work songs, one learns how to make the load lighter. My great-grandfather once told me, "Son, you know, only the gods know how to work work." It took me a long time to figure that out.

The intense, very special work songs that we sang on the railroads and in the cotton fields were meant to "work work." If one did not understand how to work work, work would work the worker to death. This was the cruelty of slave labor. Now you see the unique African American adaptation of rhythm in the search for harmony. Our sojourn here gave new meaning to the traditional African forms of the spiritual experience. Whether we hammer, or hoe, whoop or holler, or, as they say, "Slap five up high, down low, you're too slow," we do it with the rhythmic motif that leads to harmony. Possession is only the most complete form of the same rhythmic drive.

In any good blues or jazz club you can get the same soulful sound as you get in the African American church. Christianity claims the experience, but the motif, the rhythm, the feeling, the transcendence occurs anywhere the conditions present themselves. That is to say, it does not depend on icons of faith but on the incessant collective drive of a people for harmony with self, fellow earthlings, and nature. The lack of this incessant drive causes the breakdown of the traditional harmonies, because rhythmic tension must be maintained to produce harmony. Jazz is our "classical" music precisely because it contains the riffs, the counterpoints, the polyrhythms, and syncopation essential to the experience. Therefore, our orature, which is more important in many respects than our literature, is best served, and serves best, when it is influenced by jazz.

Wynton Marsalis, the noted jazz and concert musician, wrote of jazz in the following way:

> It is the most modern and profound expression of the way Black people look at the world. It is not like what Black people did in sports, where they *reinterpreted* the way the game could be played, bringing new dimensions to competitive expression in boxing, basketball and so forth. Jazz is something Negroes *invented* and it said the most profound things not only about us and the way we look at things, but about what modern democratic life is really about. It is the nobility of the race put into sound; it is the sensuousness of romance in our dialect; it is the picture of the people in all their glory, which is what swinging is.[36]

Marsalis captures the freedom, the swinging, the icon of African American music in both his music and his essaying about black music. A people oppressed and discriminated against created a liberated and free thought. This is the essence of the Afrocentric ideal as expressed in African American culture. Oratory and poetry, like music, contain the same qualities of freedom and transcendence.

In this oratorical poetry, as in music, as in all the rhythms that lead us to the complete harmony from which comes our transcendence, we are never alone. It is like prayer; we never quite understand praying alone. Since possession involves polyrhythms, we must understand that possession is always accompanied. The Jeruserema dancers of Zimbabwe, like the Adowa dancers of Ghana, never dance alone. It is neither honorable nor possible. One must not dance alone; if one *does* dance alone, the villagers would cry "Witch!" Thus, if we want to dance, we must go outside where the people are to dance, so powerful and predictable are the rhythms. Let me also say that Julius Erving, "Dr. J.," is called "Poetry in Motion" mainly because in his style of basketball he seeks to attain harmony.

One of the most interesting facts about this search for transcendence is that although it is not calculated, but rhythmic, the rhythms change, move, flow towards harmony. Many times, sitting in a jazz club, listening to a musician, you might say, "Wow, how did he do that?" It is the same with athletes, who can "switch up" in terms of their movements but still be right in time with the rhythm. The way we learn to do that is to provide for the time what is not necessarily there; this is the essence of scatting, syncopation, possession.

Cultural analysts must learn that the verbal possession, rightfully belonging to every person, will assist us as we move to harmony through rhythms that are the African path to transcendence, the only true meeting of circles and lines, the curvilinear reality of human discourse.

Notes

A note on the pictorial elements of this book: we have used Akan symbols and ideograms to open the sections of the book. For readers who are not acquainted with them, they are briefly identified here. Dancing between Circles and Lines—Ntésié (or Maté-masié), the ideogram of knowledge, is linked with the oral tradition. The knowledgeable person is one who listens well to the seers and retains everything.

Part I, The Situation—Sankofa signifies the search for knowledge, which results from diligent research and, particularly, exploration of original sources. In Akan culture, one can always return to the source to remedy error.

Part II, The Resistance—Gye Nyame signifies fearlessness. One chooses to say, "I will go this way," regardless of the obstacles.

Part III, The Liberation—Nkyimkyim signifies liberation or changing one's self. The Akan idea of freedom rests in the belief that each person can influence destiny.

Dancing between Circles and Lines

1. Raymond Geuss, *The Idea of a Critical Theory* (Cambridge: Cambridge University Press, 1984), p. 2.

2. Countee Cullen, "To Make a Poet Black" (phonodisc), read by Ruby Dee and Ossie Davis (New York: Caedrion Press, 1972).

3. Molefi K. Asante, *Afrocentricity: The Theory of Social Change* (Buffalo: Amulefi, 1980). The argument of this volume is essentially a

197

sort of congruence position. I maintain that African Americans can never achieve their full psychological potential until they find congruence between who they are and what their environment says ought to be. To be Afrocentric is to place Africans and the interest of Africa at the center of our approach to problem solving.

4. Leslie Fiedler, *Love and Death in the American Novel* (New York: Stein and Day, 1966).

5. Charles R. Larson, "Heroic Ethnocentrism: The Idea of Universality in Literature," *American Scholar* 42, no. 3 (Summer 1973): 463–467.

6. Ibid., p. 465.

7. Cedric X (Clark), D. Phillip McGee, Wade Nobles, and Luther X (Weems), "Voodoo or Io: An Introduction to African Psychology," *Journal of Black Psychology* 1, no. 2 (February 1975): 10. Another brilliant scholar in African psychology is Joseph A. Baldwin of Florida A&M University. Baldwin has contended that to speak of "Black people and Black experience outside of the context of African culture and African experience is utterly meaningless." See Joseph A. Baldwin, "African (Black) Psychology," *Journal of Black Studies* 16, no. 3 (March 1986): 241. Baldwin believes that African psychology is an affirmation of centrality in the natural order.

8. Robert Plant Armstrong, *Wellspring: On the Myth and Source of Culture* (Berkeley: University of California Press, 1975), p. 14.

9. Karen Sacks, *Sisters and Wives* (Westport, Conn.: Greenwood Press, 1979), p. 3.

10. Ibid., p. 4.

11. Molefi K. Asante and Abdulai S. Vandi, eds., *Contemporary Black Thought* (Beverly Hills: Sage Publications, 1981). See particularly the introduction.

12. Thomas Kuhn, *The Structure of Scientific Revolution* (Berkeley: University of California Press, 1970).

13. In Imre Lakatos and Alan Musgrave, eds., *Criticism and the Growth of Knowledge* (London: Cambridge University Press, 1970).

14. P. Munro, *A Brief Course in the History of Education* (London: Macmillan, 1912), p. 8.

15. W. Quill, *Subjective Psychology* (New York: Spartan Books, 1972), p. 4.

16. Marvin Harris, *Cultural Materialism: The Struggle for a Science of Culture* (New York: Random House, 1979).

17. Ibid., p. 28.

18. Ibid.
19. In Asante, *Afrocentricity*, p. 67.
20. David R. Burgest, *Social Work Practices of Minorities* (Metuchen, N.J.: Scarecrow Press, 1982).

Part 1. The Situation

1. Quoted in Jeremy Campbell, *Grammatical Man* (New York: Simon and Schuster, 1982), p. 179.
2. Paulo Freire, *The Politics of Education* (Hadley, Mass.: Bergin and Garvey, 1985).
3. Paul Rosenthal, "The Concept of Paramessage in Persuasive Communication," *Quarterly Journal of Speech* 58 (1970): 15–30.
4. Lloyd Bitzer, "The Rhetorical Situation," *Philosophy and Rhetoric* 1, (1968), pp. 1–4.
5. See J. L. Austin, *How to Do Things with Words* (Oxford: Oxford University Press, 1955), and J. Searle, *Speech Acts* (Cambridge: Cambridge University Press, 1970).
6. Haki Madhubuti, *Earthquakes and Sunrise Missions* (Chicago: Third World Press, 1984). Madhubuti conceives the objective reality of African Americans in terms of the colonial metaphor. He sees an encapsulation of the political, economic, and cultural aspirations of the African American population. In a sense, the African American is at war against capture in quite dissimilar ways than other American national cultures. Madhubuti claims an assertive cultural nationalism as the only approach to intellectual and cultural liberation.
7. P. Daudi, "The Discourse of Power or the Power of Discourse," *Alternatives* (1983), p. 276.
8. Ibid., p. 277.
9. A. Goldschlager, "Towards a Semiotics of Authoritarian Discourse," *Poetics Today* 3, no. 1 (1982): 11–13.
10. Herbert Marcuse, *One Dimensional Man: Studies in the Ideology of Advanced Industrial Society* (Boston: Beacon Press, 1964). Marcuse's technological vise is credited for the lack of creative will in both the West and the socialist nations. There is only one dimension dictated by the industrial and high-technological managed societies. A ready-made, built-in dictionary of thought and action governs the one-dimensional man.
11. Octavio Paz, *The Bow and the Lyre* (New York: McGraw-Hill, 1973).

12. Na'im Akbar, "Mental Disorder among African Americans," *Black Books Bulletin* 7, no. 2 (1981): 18–25.

13. Daudi, "Discourse," p. 274.

14. E. Buyssens, *La Communication et l'articulation linguistique* (Brussels, Presses Universitaires de Bruxelles, 1978).

15. Daudi, "Discourse," p. 277.

16. Arthur Lovejoy, *The Great Chain of Being* (Cambridge, Mass.: Harvard University Press, 1964), p. 24.

17. Daniel Bell, "Technology, Nature and Society," *American Scholar* 42, no. 3 (Summer 1973): 391.

18. Martin Steinmann, *New Rhetorics* (New York: Scribner's, 1967).

19. In Walt Wolfram and Marcia Whitemann, "The Role of Dialect Interference in Composition," *Florida FL Reporter* (Spring–Fall 1971), pp. 34–38.

20. Steinmann, *New Rhetorics*, p. 26.

21. Henry Mitchell, *Black Preaching* (New York: Lippincott, 1970), p. 24. Mitchell's presentation of the phenomenon of black preaching underscores variety in theme, tonal quality, and rhetorical qualities. Charles V. Hamilton's *The Black Preacher in America* (New York: Morrow and Co., 1972) places the black preacher into a political context, showing the relationship of the preacher to power. Mitchell's intention, on the contrary, is the elevation of the black preacher's style of eloquence in the mind of his readers. Both views are clearly within the scope of the African American preaching tradition.

22. Vernon Dixon and Badi Foster, *Beyond Black or White* (Boston: Little, Brown, 1971).

23. Ibid., *passim*.

24. LeRoi Jones (Imamu Amiri Baraka), *Blues People* (New York: Morrow and Co., 1963), p. 26.

25. Kariamu Asante, "Commonalities in African Dance: An Aesthetic Foundation," in M. Asante and K. W. Asante, eds., *African Culture: The Rhythms of Unity* (Westport, Conn.: Greenwood Press, 1985). The commonalities identified by Kariamu Asante in the traditional dance of Africa are found in music, religion, and relationships as well. Indeed, the thesis of *African Culture* is the idea that Africa presents one vast cultural river with numerous tributaries. Polyrhythm, according to Kariamu Asante, represents one of the seven principal senses of African aesthetics.

26. Henry Mitchell, *Black Preaching* (New York: Lippincott, 1970), p. 162.

27. See Jones, *Blues People*, p. 31.

28. Henry Highland Garnet, "An Address to the Slave," in Arthur Smith and Stephen Robb, *The Voice of Black Rhetoric* (Boston: Allyn & Bacon, 1970), pp. 22–32.

29. Malcolm X and George Breitman, *Malcolm X Speaks* (New York: Grove Press, 1966)

30. David Walker, "An Appeal to the Colored Citizens of the World," in Herbert Aptheker, *One Continual Cry* (New York: Humanities Press, 1965).

31. James Weldon Johnson, *God's Trombones* (New York: Viking, 1965), pp. 1–3.

32. Charles V. Hamilton, *The Black Preacher in America* (New York: William Morrow, 1972), p. 42.

33. Mitchell, *Black Preaching*, p. 14.

34. Jones, *Blues People*, p. 26.

35. A version of the signifying monkey I learned as a child in Nashville, Tennessee.

36. Paul Carter Harrison, *The Drama of Nommo* (New York: Grove Press, 1972), p. 48.

37. Janheinz Jahn, *Muntu: The New African Culture* (New York: Grove Press, 1961), pp. 170–173.

38. Ibid., p. 174.

39. Malcolm X, "Message from the Grass Roots." Record Album. (New York: Douglas Communications, n.d.).

40. Melville Herskovits, *The Myth of the Negro Past* (Boston: Beacon Press, 1958), p. 156.

41. Ibid., p. 158.

42. See Robert Farris Thompson, *Black Gods and Kings* (Bloomington: Indiana University Press, 1971), pp. 3–4, for a discussion of African art, symbolism, and society. Thompson's work seeks to provide an objective African interpretation of culture. In *The Flash of the Spirit* (New York: Random House, 1983), for example, he is content to allow the indigenous cultures of Africa to provide their own explanations of African art. In many ways Thompson follows the tradition begun by Melville Herskovits and the Northwestern School.

43. Eleanor W. Traylor, "The Fabulous World of Toni Morrison," in Amiri Baraka and Amina Baraka (eds.), *Confirmations* (New York: Quill, 1983), pp. 342–343.

44. Armstrong, *Wellspring*, pp. 102–103.

45. Ibid.

46. Ibid., p. 107.

47. B. L. Bailey, "Language and Communication Styles in Afro-American Children in the United States," *Florida FL Reporter* 7 (Spring/Summer 1969): 46.

48. R. G. Kaplan, "On a Note of Protest (in a Minor Key): Bidialectism vs. Bidialectism," *Florida FL Reporter* (Spring/Summer 1969).

49. Thompson, *The Flash of the Spirit*, p. 228.

50. Ibid., p. 229.

51. Michael Bradley, *The Iceman Inheritance* (Toronto: Dorset, 1979).

52. Armstrong, *Wellspring*, p. 24.

53. See Hilda Kuper and Leo Kuper, eds., *African Law: Adaptation and Development* (Los Angeles: University of California Press, 1965).

54. Paul Bohannan, *Justice and Judgment among the Tiv* (London: Oxford University Press, 1957), p. 6.

55. Adebayo Adesanya, "Yoruba Metaphysical Thinking," *ODU* (Ibadan) 5 (1958): 39. Word power is not merely a Yoruba cultural phenomenon, it is the tradition of most African societies. The Ibo, the Ga, the Akan, all possess the same appreciation of the power of the word. Nothing exists without speech. To know something, it must be spoken, and in speech one has a relationship with other humans.

56. Wole Soyinka, *Ake: The Years of Childhood* (London: Rex Collings, 1981).

57. Alan Merriam, "African Music," in William Bascom and Melville Herskovits, *Continuity and Change in African Culture* (Chicago: University of Chicago Press, 1958), p. 49.

58. See Leonard Barrett, *Soul Force* (Garden City, N.Y.: Anchor Press, 1974).

59. Melville Herskovits, *Man and His Works* (New York: Knopf, 1948), p. 379.

60. Abu Abarry, "Rhetoric and Poetics of Oral African Literature: A Study of the Ga of Ghana" (unpublished dissertation, SUNY-Buffalo, 1977), p. 76.

61. Walter J. Ong, *The Presence of the Word* (New York: Simon and Schuster, 1970), pp. 17–27.

62. Ibid., p. 16.

63. Jahn, *Muntu*, p. 134.

64. Ibid., p. 133.

65. For instance, Leopold Senghor, "Der geist der Negro Afrikanischen Kultur," in *Schwarze Ballade*, ed. Janheinz Jahn (Frankfurt: Verlag, 1965), pp. 203–227.
66. Klaus Wachsmann, "Ethnomusicology in Africa," in *The African Experience*, ed. John Paden and Edward Soja (Evanston, Ill.: Northwestern University Press, 1970), p. 135.
67. Michael Appiah, "Okyeame: The Akan Communication System" (unpublished dissertation, SUNY-Buffalo, 1979), p. 76.
68. Ibid., p. 76.
69. H. Rap Brown, "Rap's Poem," in Stephen Henderson, *Understanding of the New Black Poetry* (New York: Morrow, 1973), p. 187.
70. Appiah, "Okyeame: The Akan Communication System," p. 81.

Part 2.   The Resistance

1. See Jahn, *Muntu*, pp. 121–156, and W. E. B. Du Bois, *The Souls of Black Folk* (New York: Fawcett, 1961), pp. 15–22.
2. Benjamin Brawley, *The Negro Genius* (New York, 1937), pp. 5–21.
3. Jahn, *Muntu*, pp. 128–131.
4. See Melville J. Herskovits, "The Contribution of Afro-American Studies to Africanist Research," *American Anthropologist* 50 (January–March 1948): 1–10; Merle Eppse, *The Negro, Too, in American History* (New York, 1938), p. 70; LeRoi Jones (Imamu Amiri Baraka), *Blues People* (New York: Morrow, 1963), pp. 43–49, and *Black Music* (New York: Morrow, 1968), pp. 182–83. Additional information can be found in Melville J. Herskovits, "African Literature," in *Encyclopedia of Literature*, ed. Joseph T. Shipley (New York, 1946), 1:3–15, and Richard A. Waterman and William R. Bascom, "African and New World Negro Folklore," in *Funk and Wagnalls Standard Dictionary of Folklore, Mythology, and Legend*, ed. Maria Leach (New York, 1949), 1:18–24.
5. Jahn, *Muntu*, p. 230. A much broader view is provided by Leopold Sedar Senghor, "The Spirit of Civilization or the Laws of African Negro Culture," *Presence Africaine*, nos. 8–10 (June–November 1956), p. 58.
6. Carter C. Woodson, *Negro Orators and Their Orations* (Washington, D.C.: Associated Publishers, 1925). Woodson is principally known for his classic discussion of African American education, *The Miseducation of the Negro*, but also as a proponent of African history. As founder of Black History commemorations and the Association for the Study of Black Life and Culture, he, more than anyone, revolu-

tionized the thinking about African history. *Negro Orators and Their Orations* is his contribution to the oral traditions of African American history.

7. See Eppse; Willim Ferris, *African Abroad* (New Haven, Conn.: Tuttle, Morehouse and Taylor, 1913); and C. Eric Lincoln, *Sounds of the Struggle: Persons and Perspectives in Civil Rights* (New York: Morrow, 1967).

8. Such outstanding nineteenth-century orators as Samuel Ringgold Ward, Reverdy Ransom, and Henry Highland Garnet were products of the religious schools and theological seminaries.

9. The work of poets such as Paul Laurence Dunbar, Fenton Johnson, Jean Toomer, and Langston Hughes can be found in Arna Bontemps, ed., *American Negro Poetry* (New York: Harcourt, Brace and World, 1963).

10. See Edmund David Cronon, *Black Moses* (Madison: University of Wisconsin Press, 1968), pp. 209–219.

11. Quoted in Woodson, *Negro Orators*, p. 37.

12. See Arthur L. Smith (M. K. Asante), *Rhetoric of Black Revolution* (Boston: Allyn & Bacon, 1969), p. 34. I identified villification, objectification, legitimation, and mythication as strategies of protest in this book.

13. Jones, *Blues People*, p. xi.

14. Marcel Griaule, *Conversations with Ogotommêli* (London: Oxford University Press, 1965).

15. Harrison, *The Drama of Nommo*, p. 67.

16. Oswald Spengler, *The Decline of the West*, Vol. I (New York: Knopf, 1932), p. 189.

17. C. G. Jung, Bruno Bettleheim, and Joseph Campbell, among others, have explored the value of symbolic interactions with mystery for individual psyches, as well as the mental health of societies.

18. Claude Lévi-Strauss, *The Raw and the Cooked* (New York: Harper and Row, 1970), p. 12.

19. Armstrong, *Wellspring*.

20. Isidore Okpewho, "Poetry and Pattern: Structural Analysis of an Ijo Creation Myth," *Journal of American Folkfore* 92, no. 365, (July–September 1979): 302–324.

21. Ibid., p. 304.

22. Ibid., p. 305.

23. Herskovits, *The Myth of the Negro Past*.

24. This version of Shine is from south Georgia. I first heard it in 1950 in Valdosta.

25. Melvin Dixon, "Singing Swords: The Literary Legacy of Slavery," in Charles T. Davis and Henry Louis Gates Jr., *The Slave's Narrative* (New York: Oxford University Press, 1985), p. 305.

26. See Molefi Asante and Abdulai Vandi, eds., *Contemporary Black Thought: Alternatives in the Social Sciences* (Beverly Hills, Calif.: Sage Publications, 1979). See also the chapters by Joseph Baldwin and Dona Richards. Baldwin discusses what happens to a people's psychology under oppression; Richards shows how the idea of progress serves the Europeans' domination of African people.

27. In A. Smith (M. Asante) and Stephen Robb, *The Voice of Black Rhetoric* (Boston: Allyn & Bacon, 1971), p. 202.

28. In ibid., p. 83.

29. Armstrong, *Wellspring*, p. 94.

30. Ibid.

31. John Illo, "The Rhetoric of Malcolm X," *Columbia University Forum* 9 (Spring 1966): 10.

32. H. Rap Brown, *Die, Nigger, Die* (New York: Dial Press, 1960), p. 29.

33. In Smith and Robb, *Voice of Black Rhetoric*, p. 131.

34. Ibid., p. 240.

35. Benjamin Mays, in ibid., p. 298.

36. Erwin Bettinghaus, *Persuasive Communication* (New York: Holt, Rinehart & Winston, 1968), p. 37.

37. Aimé Césaire, *The Collected Poetry* (Berkeley: University of California Press, 1983).

38. Robert Pirsig, *Zen and the Art of Motorcycle Maintenance* (New York: Bantam Books, 1972), p. 275.

39. Frantz Fanon, *The Wretched of the Earth* (New York: Grove, 1968). In the end, Fanon sees the specter of a neo-colonialism in which those who were oppressed and who resisted their oppression often become oppressors themselves. Only in the avoidance of this cycle does the "new human" break the European tradition of killing man while talking about the "new man."

40. John Illo, "The Rhetoric of Malcolm X," p. 5.

41. Mitchell, *Black Preaching*.

42. Garnet, "An Address to the Slave," pp. 22–32.

43. Frederick Douglass, *My Bondage and My Freedom* (New York: Arno Press and New York Times, 1968), p. 441.

44. Ibid.

45. Houston Baker, Jr., *Blues: Ideology and Afro-American Litera-*

ture: A Vernacular Theory (Chicago: University of Chicago Press, 1984). Baker's illuminating work should also be read as a treatise on the significance of the folk motif in the creation of African American verbal art.

46. W. E. B. Du Bois, *The Souls of Black Folks* (New York: Fawcett, 1961), p. 16. The entire corpus of Du Bois' work dealt with the idea of double consciousness, the fact that the African in America existed in two separate realities. This thesis has been critiqued, however, in terms of choice—that is, the possibility that an individual may choose to have a single consciousness.

47. James Cone, *Spirituals and the Blues* (New York: Seabury Press, 1972), p. 16.

48. Yet Du Bois moved to Africa and died in Ghana in 1963. The government of Ghana, under Kwame Nkrumah, accorded him its highest citizen honor. In 1986 the government of Ghana, under Jerry Rawlings, dedicated a memorial center in honor of Du Bois.

49. Anthony Appiah, "The Uncompleted Argument: Du Bois and the Illusion of Race," *Critical Inquiry* (Autumn 1985), p. 27.

50. Ibid., p. 28.

51. Henry Louis Gates Jr., "Writing, Race and the Difference It Makes," *Critical Inquiry* (Autumn 1985), pp. 10–11.

52. Ibid., p. 11.

53. Ibid., p. 12.

54. See Du Bois, *The Souls of Black Folks.*

55. See Asante, *Afrocentricity*, pp. 20–21.

56. Appiah, "Uncompleted Argument," p. 36.

57. See Arthur L. Smith (M. K. Asante), *Rhetoric of Black Revolution.*

58. Peter I. Rose, ed., *Americans from Africa: Old Memories, New Moods* (New York: Atherton Press, 1970), p. 79. I have quoted all Nat Turner comments from this text.

59. Ibid., p. 79.

60. Ibid.

61. Ibid.

62. Ibid, p. 81.

63. Ibid.

64. Ibid., p. 82.

65. Albert Murray, *The Omni-Americans* (New York: Vintage Press, 1970).

66. Ibid.

67. Ibid., p. 83.

68. Ibid.

69. Ibid., p. 84.

70. Ibid., p. 79.

71. Ibid., p. 80.

72. Ibid., p. 79.

73. See particularly Marie Hochmuth and Norman Mattis, "Phillips Brooks," and Willard Hayes Yeager, "Wendell Phillips," both in William Norwood Brigance, ed., *A History and Criticism of American Public Address* (New York: Russell and Russell, 1960), 1:294–328 and 329–362, respectively.

74. Indeed, the stage of rhetoric and public address in the Western world has been set without consideration of African orators. What has often appeared is a sort of institutional racism in criticism, a "house criticism" limited to white politicians' rhetoric. This means, of course, that Prince Saunders, John Langston, George White, and Henry Garnet—among numerous other black speakers—have seldom been examined by American scholars. While it is possible for a critic to comment on the rhetorical skills and talents of a Webster, Phillips, or Sumner, one can never be sure that criticism has taken into consideration all the possibilities within a given rhetorical situation. One gets a certain *déjà vu* feeling that the problem of a Eurocentric frame of reference finds its expression in communication as it does in other fields.

75. Lerone Bennett, *Before the Mayflower* (Baltimore: Penguin Books, 1966), pp. 141–152.

76. Unlike many black preachers of his day, Garnet had the benefit of seminary training in homiletics. For the role of the seminary in training black preachers, see W. E. B. Du Bois, *The Negro Church* (Atlanta: Atlanta University Press, 1903); Benjamin Mays, *The Negro Church* (New York: Russell and Russell, 1969); and E. Franklin Frazier, *The Negro Church in America* (New York: Schocken Books, 1963).

77. Herbert Aptheker, *One Continual Cry* (New York: Humanities Press, 1965), p. 38.

78. Ibid.

79. Ibid.

80. Ibid.

81. Woodson, *Negro Orators and Their Orations*, p. 312.

82. Thomas Frazier, ed., *Afro-American Primary Sources* (New York: Harcourt, Brace and World, 1970), p. 114.

83. Ibid.

84. Ibid.

85. Ibid., p. 115.

86. Aptheker, *One Continual Cry*, p. 69.

87. Frazier, *Afro-American Primary Sources*, p. 116.

88. Woodson, *Negro Orators*, p. 312.

89. Ibid., p. 117.

90. Ibid., p. 118.

91. Ibid., p. 119.

92. Henry H. Garnet, *Walker's Appeal and Garnet's Address to the Slaves of the United States* (New York: J. H. Tobbitt, 1848).

93. Aptheker, *One Continual Cry*, p. 40.

94. See R. L. Davis to William Coppinger, August 31, 1891, American Colonization Society Papers, Manuscript Division, Library of Congress, Washington, D.C., p. 2.

95. Amy Jacques-Garvey, ed., *The Philosophy and Opinions of Marcus Garvey* (New York: Atheneum, 1968), p. 49.

96. Ibid., p. 57.

97. In Edwin Redkey, *Black Exodus* (New Haven: Yale University Press, 1969), p. 33.

98. Smith (Asante), *Rhetoric of Black Revolution*, p. 34.

99. Redkey, *Black Exodus*, p. 24.

100. Ibid., p. 25.

101. Thaddeus E. Horton, "A Black Moses," in James T. Haley, ed., *Afro-American Encyclopedia* (Nashville, 1895), pp. 35–38.

102. *Atlanta Constitution*, September 4, 1868.

103. Redkey, *Black Exodus*, p. 27.

104. Ibid., p. 29.

105. Edmund Cronon, *Black Moses* (Madison: University of Wisconsin Press, 1968), p. 66.

106. Ibid., p. 99.

107. Ibid.

108. Ibid., p. 142.

109. The Afrocentricist makes a distinction between blackness as a biological condition and blackness as a philosophical or ideological position. One is reminded of Martin Kilson's unfortunate essay, "The Paradoxes of Blackness: Notes on the Crisis of Black Intellectuals," which appeared in *Dissent* in February 1986. Kilson confuses *blackness* with *black people*; but *blackness*, as he wants to use the term, is a philosophical perspective. Such a perspective, like other

perspectives, is hammered out of the existential encounters of those who articulate it.

110. From time to time, separationists have tried to persuade blacks to settle in countries other than those in Africa; they have failed dismally. In Kansas, Colonel John M. Brown, a black politician, advocated Brazil as the Afro-Americans' new home. Although his plans for taking blacks to Brazil were elaborate, he had little success in raising money and even less in raising black passions. William Ellis, a black businessman in Texas, attempted to start a Mexican colony in 1889 to raise cotton and coffee, but despite support from the Mexican legislature, he gained almost no support among blacks. (See *Christian Recorder*, November 7, 1889; *Savannah Tribune*, October 19, 1889.) Africans did settle in the West Indies—but only Africa has had a galvanizing effect upon the black community.

111. Garvey, *Marcus*, p. 97.

112. Redkey, *Black Exodus*, p. 29.

113. *Voice of Missions*, August 1895.

Part 3. The Liberation

1. Edmund Husserl, *The Crisis of European Sciences* (Evanston, Ill.: Northwestern University Press, 1935).

2. Jean-Paul Sartre, *Critique de la raison dialectique* (Paris: Gallimard, 1960).

3. Ibid., p. 138.

4. Ibid., p. 140.

5. Ibid., pp. 140–144.

6. Claude Lévi-Strauss, *The Savage Mind* (Chicago: University of Chicago Press, 1966), p. 247. In this book, Lévi-Strauss tries to distance himself from the conceptions of Malinowski and Levy-Bruhl. Malinowski was quite unabashedly a functionalist. He believed that social institutions could be explained by how people found subsistence, satisfied their sexual drives, and sheltered themselves from the environment. On the other hand, Levy-Bruhl believed that Africans and Asians used intuition and affection as the bases of their thought processes. This "emotional" conceptualization and Malinowski's utilitarian conceptualization were rejected by Lévi-Strauss, who opted for structuralism, which he argued was based on order and rules.

7. Sartre, *Critique*, p. 183.

8. Lévi-Strauss, *Savage Mind*, p. 249.

9. LeRoi Jones (Imamu Amiri Baraka), *Home* (New York: Grove Press, 1969), p. 246.

10. Ngugi wa Thiong'o, *Decolonising the Mind* (London: Currey, 1981), p. 3.

11. Carlton Molette and Barbara Molette, *Black Theatre: Premise and Presentation* (Bristol, Ind.: Wyndham Hall Press, 1986), p. 91. They have defined African American theater in terms that have been employed by Afrocentricists regarding research and information; that is, they have rejected the notion that the simple treatment of African themes constitutes an Afrocentric theater.

12. Ibid., p. 92.

13. Michel Foucault, *Madness and Civilization* (New York: Random House, 1965). p. 6.

14. Ibid., pp. 23–36. One might look to Foucault's other works, such as *Power/Knowledge: Selected Interviews and Other Writings, 1972–77* (New York: Pantheon, 1981), and *The Archaeology of Knowledge* (New York: Harper and Row, 1976), for elaboration on the intellectual development of the West.

15. Jack Daniel and Geneva Smitherman, "How I Got Ovah: Communication Dynamics in the Black Community," *Quarterly Journal of Speech* 62, no. 1 (February 1976): 26–39.

16. Leon Phillips, "A Comparative Study of Two Approaches for Analyzing Black Discourse" (unpublished dissertation, 1983, Howard University).

17. Murray, *The Omni-Americans*, pp. 1–15.

18. Ibid., p. 82.

19. There are numerous works that emphasize the value of the concept of harmony in African culture. For example, Wade Nobles, *African Psychology* (Oakland, Calif.: Black Family Institute Publications, 1986); Amos Wilson, *The Developmental Psychology of the Black Child* (New York: United Brothers Communication Systems, 1978); Leachim Semaj, *Culture, Africanity, and Male/Female Relationships: Working Papers on Cultural Science* (Ithaca, N.Y.: Cornell University Press, 1980); Jacob Carruthers, *Essays in Ancient Egyptian Studies* (Los Angeles: University of Sankore Press, 1984); and Molefi Asante, "*Ma'at:* The African Way against Injustice and Chaos," paper presented to First World Forum, New York, New York, October 25, 1986. The latter represents a selected part of the corpus of work being done

on the concept of harmony as *ma'at*, as *nommo*, as *dja*, and as a relative to Ifa.

20. See Maulana Karenga, "Black Studies and the Problematic of Paradigm: The Philosophical Dimension," *Phylon*, forthcoming; James Turner, "Foreword: Africana Studies and Epistemology: A Discourse in the Sociology of Knowledge," in James E. Turner, ed., *The Next Decade: Theoretical and Research Issues in Africana Studies* (Ithaca, N.Y.: Cornell University African Research Center, 1985), pp. v–xxv; and James B. Stewart, "The Legacy of W. E. B. Du Bois for Contemporary Black Studies," *Journal of Negro Education* (Summer 1984), pp. 296–311.

21. Stewart, "Legacy of W. E. B. Du Bois," pp. 296–311.

22. Karenga, "Black Studies and the Problematic of Paradigm."

23. See Asante, *Afrocentricity*. Karenga has correctly noted that my definition of Afrocentricity is descriptive, but there is no problem with description in the context of my analysis in *Afrocentricity: The Theory of Social Change*, because that work was itself a kind of *praxis* and was meant to be used as *praxis*, thereby rendering description not only valid but necessary. Nevertheless, I had explained elsewhere that Afrocentricity is a perspective that recognizes the centrality of Africa as a starting point for analysis and synthesis. See, for example, Molefi K. Asante, "Intercultural Communication: An Afrocentric Inquiry into Encounter," in Bruce Williams and Orlando Taylor, eds., *International Conference on Black Communication: A Bellagio Conference* (New York: Rockefeller Foundation, 1978).

24. Asante, "Intercultural Communication," p. 16.

25. Karenga, "Black Studies."

26. Turner, *The Next Decade*, p. xxviii.

27. W. Van Dusen, *The Presence of Other Worlds: The Findings of Emmanuel Swedenborg* (New York: Harper, 1974).

28. Jahn, *Muntu*, pp. 11–14.

29. Wande Abimbola, *Ifa Divination Poetry* (New York: Nok, 1973), p. 3.

30. Ibid., p. 3.

31. Ibid.

32. See Jordan Ngubane, *The Conflict of Minds* (New York: Books in Focus, 1979). Ngubane brings to the study of African philosophy an Afrocentric understanding of the relationship of the Zulu to the universe that reminds one of the ancient Kemetic concept of *ma'at*.

Since all African philosophical thought finds roots in the classical civilizations of antiquity, the "*sudic* ideal" in Ngubane's work is akin to the concepts of *ma'at, dja, nommo,* and even the African American transformation as soul. They are integral to an understanding and appreciation of the African world voice.

33. Dona Richards, "The Implications of African American Spirituality," in M. Asante and K. Welsh Asante, *African Culture: The Rhythms of Unity* (Westport, Conn.: Greenwood Press, 1985). Richards sees this collective sense in many African behaviors, for example, when we say "We are family" or when we say we "partied," as an indication of the *sudic* ideal. She writes that "the essence of the African cosmos is spiritual reality; that is its fundamental nature, its primary essence" (p. 210).

34. Ibid.

35. Roy Bhaskar, *A Realist Theory of Science* (Atlantic Highlands, N.J.: Humanities Press, 1975).

36. Wynton Marsalis, "Why We Must Preserve Our Jazz Heritage," *Ebony* (February 1986), p. 131.

Index

213